Tales of a
Traveling Coffeepreneuer

A Journey to Find the World's Best Coffee

By

Anthony Harding

First Edition

Special Thanks

If it wasn't for the many people who have been there to support me, I wouldn't be who I am today. Now that I have finished writing my first book and I work through the halls of entrepreneurship on a mission to become one of the G.O.A.T.S. I want every one of you to know how happy and grateful I am to have had you there to teach and support me along the way.

I don't think I could have done it without any of you. I want to thank some of the people who were instrumental in my journey. If I leave you out, I want you to know that the value you have added to my life is definitely not lost on me. I am eternally grateful for everything you helped me with along the way.

Thank you and I love you.

Special Thanks to:

My Dad. With all the crap life has dealt you over the years. And everything I piled on top of that. Thank you for sticking by me and being patient with me and allowing me to mold myself into who I am today. You are my biggest influence and inspiration in life and my greatest teacher. I hope that in your eyes it has all paid off.

My Mom. Our relationship has been rocky over the years. Yet, whenever I was in a place where I was losing my mental shit, you miraculously appeared to be the rock I needed. I am grateful for that. Thank you

Cheryl. Thank you for always being there for me throughout my life. You mean more to me than you will ever know.

The late great Dimebag Darrell. Your music started me on the path that would lead me to where I am today. You were the last person who got me drunk, and the day you were murdered was the day I stopped smoking weed. Your death inspired me to move into the music industry and find myself in a state where I would become suicidal. Most would think this was a bad thing, but that led me to take my spiritual journey. Sadly, I don't think can ever return the favor to you, but until we drink again, Rock in Paradise, my friend.

Kyle Cease. Thank you for showing me how to access my true being and how to navigate past being comfortable. If you didn't start evolving, you wouldn't have made the video that talked me out of killing myself. There is no way to thank you enough for that alone. And beyond that, challenging me to get involved with Evolving Out Loud. By pushing yourself, and being present with me, you pushed me to work on becoming my highest possible self. I'm nowhere near that at this point in my life. But I wouldn't be anywhere near where I am today had it not been for you inspiring me. It's hard to believe we've known each other for almost 16 years.

Audrey Griffin. You have been the girl of my dreams for nearly a decade. Our story has been a rollercoaster. However, if it wasn't for you, I wouldn't have learned the patience to become a world-traveling entrepreneur. No matter where our journeys take us and how far apart from each other we are, you will always be the love of my life. Thank you for introducing me to The Secret and meditation and a lot of other things that I'm not going to mention. I love you.

Amy Gerrits. You are my best friend. You have pushed me to a mental level (more than anyone I know) on a daily basis for over 20 years. You've been my sounding board. The person who made me look at myself when I was a whiny little bitch, freaking out over temporary circumstances. And I could go on and on for months with this list of things you have done for me. Thank you and I love you.

Thuy Vu, Lance Wrzesinski, Hirsh Diamant, Lee Coumbs. You are the greatest teachers and mentors a student could ever ask for. Without you, none of what I have accomplished would have ever taken place. I cannot extend the amount of gratitude I hold in my heart for all four of you, through the written word. Thank you.

5

Yendor Senyah. Thanks for being my comic relief over the years and my brother. You have always been in my corner and the spot of darkness in my positivity that I kept close to even out my duality. You've always made me look at things a second time to make sure I did it correctly. I am truly grateful.

Chanel Schock. The best roommate I ever had. If it wasn't for you, I wouldn't have been sitting in the coffee shop as often as I was. And none of this would have played out this way. Thank you for always being there for me, and for Gus. I love you and Jayden, who has helped out in immeasurable ways as well. Thank you.

Linda Foss. You taught me how to write, and the work you did for me during the editing process was invaluable to me, and I don't think I could have made this book happen without you.

Cameron Daniels. You have become my coffee sensei. You have helped me so much along my journey to becoming a coffeepreneur. Here is to many more years of friendship and annoying you from time to time. Love you bro. To the readers, definitely check out Phantom Coffee Roasters from Lacey Washington. Cameron is a genius and his coffee is amazing.

Table of Contents

Introduction

Four years before I finished writing this book, I was only a few months away from figuring out that I had a passion for coffee and tea. I was three years into the beginning stages of a spiritual and an educational journey that all began with me nearly committing suicide.

I decided to write this book for a number of different reasons. One, I've been on a lot of journeys around the world and I know a lot of people are interested in hearing those stories. Two, through my coffee journey, I've come to realize that most people know very little about coffee. It wasn't long ago that I was one of those people. But the most important reason was that I wanted to show people that no matter how bad the circumstances you might be going through at any given moment, it isn't too late to change course and go out and live your dreams.

By writing this book, I offer to you hope in yourself that you too can start traveling the world, doing the things you have always said "someday" about. I want you to know that even if you are in a state of mind thinking nobody is in your corner, or nobody believes in you, I believe in you and I am in your corner.

That being said, my name is Anthony Harding. I was born in Sheridan, Wyoming. When I was in the first grade, my father became a paraplegic and was soon raising two kids as a single father who couldn't walk. Life was hard growing up, but for the most part, I never lost faith that I was going to be someone. As I write this today, I have four degrees, and I've set foot in fifteen countries on four continents. I've met literally 1000's of celebrities. I've started five different businesses over the years ranging from candy, drugs, music, celebrity memorabilia, and now the coffee and tea business.

As you can see, I've lived a very interesting life, and this book is just a short little clip of it. Hopefully, by putting in the effort of writing it, I can inspire you to grab life by the horns, and live it to the fullest.

> Thank You Very Much,
> The Traveling Coffepreneuer
> Anthony Harding

Chapter 1

The Birth of a Coffeepreneuer

Many people will look at somebody and wonder, "Why should I listen to this person?" or "What makes this person an expert?" These are important questions to ponder when you are starting a new business, or entering a field where you intend to be an influencer. This book is about how I became an expert on coffee.

When I was growing up, I lived in a family with a brother who was eight years older than me, and my father was a single parent. It sounds like the normal middle-class American family from the 80's and 90's, but our family was a bit different than most. When I was in the first grade, about a year before my mother left my father, my dad tipped a forklift over on himself at work, crushing his lower spine and severing his spinal cord. This accident confined my father to a wheelchair for the rest of his life.

I had a troubled childhood. I refused to do my school work. It was safe to say that I really didn't care about much of anything other than trying to be happy inside of my own skin. For a good portion of my childhood, I didn't have much adult supervision because my mother didn't live with us and my father was pretty much out of his mind on pain medication. Not only was he on the pain meds, but he was also very vocal about his suicidal thoughts. It's no wonder I didn't give a shit for the most part, but I did step up where it actually mattered. My job early on was to help my father live a decent life.

I went everywhere with my father, making sure he could get into and out of his wheelchair and helping him at the grocery store or wherever he needed to be in public. I also cleaned up accidents of incontinence when necessary.

Eventually, he developed pressure sores, and I had to learn to do the job of a wound therapist. Because of my father's advanced case, by the time I was 13 years old, I had become one of the best wound therapists in Washington State. It was terrible...

When I was in the 8th grade I started my first business. I realized that the other students in my school all loved candy and it was hard to come by at school. There was a wholesale store a few blocks away from my house where I could buy a 300-piece bag of Jolly Rancher bite-sized candies for $3. So, I bought a bag, took it to school, and began selling them for a quarter each. As soon as the word got out, I would consistently sell out of candy by lunch period. It didn't take me long to start adding other products like Cry Baby Gum Balls, and fun size candy bars. I usually came home with around $75 per day. $375 per week was pretty good money for a middle school student. Sadly, once the school faculty took notice, they thought I was selling drugs out of my locker. Of course, they checked my locker and found my stash of candy. I didn't get in any trouble, but they made me stop selling the candy at school. That totally sucked.

A couple years later I did find drugs. I used the same basic formula as I did with the candy, except I didn't do the exchanges at school, but, I did set up the sales there. I started out by buying an eighth of an ounce of high-grade marijuana for $45. I would smoke half of it and break the other half into 18 tiny little buds that I would sell for $5 each. I managed to make this work for a couple months before my customers started to find other connections that didn't charge so much. But by this time, I was able to sell bigger bags like the other connections in town. It wasn't long until I found meth, mushrooms, and LSD. Once I found that stuff, I quickly became one of the most popular kids in town. I was making a ton of money, but I was partying it all away. It lasted a couple of years before I got pulled over and searched by the police just after I had turned 18 years old. They found enough LSD on me that I could have spent the next 30 years of my life in prison. Luckily, one of the officers on the scene I knew from when we were kids. He was able to talk his Sergeant into letting me go with a promise that I would walk away from that life. I did just that.

I started working minimum wage jobs; I was a used car lot attendant, a car detailer, a pizza delivery driver, I flipped burgers, and I even made screen doors. By this time I had a passion for music and I was beginning to collect music equipment. I intended to become a Heavy Metal Singer. I put together 3/4 of a band and I was having a great time screaming my lyrics, but I couldn't find a guitar player. Eventually, I realized I didn't have any idea what I was doing, so I stepped out of the way so the band could evolve, and I began learning how to manage a band.

The minimum wage life was killing me. I hated not having any money like I did in my drug-dealing days, and I absolutely hated working for other people. At the time, eBay was new on the scene, so I decided to start chasing after celebrities to sign things that I would sell on eBay. I quickly learned that this new business was very much like selling drugs. The money was beginning to roll in again, and I was beginning to make some friends in high places. After a couple of years, I began to really focus on the music industry. I was buying recording equipment, and PA equipment. It wasn't long before I produced my first CD, by a local rapper named Jonah J. I had no idea what I was doing and the quality of the audio definitely shows that. I even started a concert production company called THC Productions and started building a strong music scene in a town that didn't have a scene at all. Before long, I decided to go to audio recording school in Tempe, Arizona.

When I came back from Arizona, I pieced together a band to manage named Blood To Dust, and I used it to reinvigorate THC Productions. After about a year, I produced their album. This album was much better quality than the Jonah J album. During this time, I ended up needing an emergency surgery to remove eight inches of my colon due to a perforation of the bowel that left me with a colostomy and addicted to oxycodone. This procedure would need to be reversed after 8 months.

I was doing a great job managing the band and causing them to make enough noise in the industry that I was contacted by an Artists & Repertoire guy from a major record label. He told me he could come and see the band play, but the only date he had available was the day of my reversal surgery.

So I set up a show at Studio Seven in Seattle, Washington for the day of my surgery. Regretfully, I didn't tell the band about the A&R guy. The day after the surgery when I woke up, I received a call from the singer of the band telling me that they couldn't find our guitar player. They were unable to find him and had to cancel the show.

As a result, the band got blackballed; I got black-balled as a promoter in the big city. The state was about to pass a law privatizing alcohol sales, causing all the bars I had been working with to say they couldn't afford to pay for entertainment. My entire life that I had spent the prior decade building was gone pretty much overnight. That, combined with my newly found addiction to the oxycodone, caused me to get suicidal.

Fortunately, just as I was getting ready to do myself in, I was stopped by some divine intervention. Instead of killing myself, I enrolled in college to start studying business. I spent the next three years at Centralia College taking as many of their business classes as I could possibly take. Finally, I graduated with my AA and transferred up to The Evergreen State College.

At the end of my first quarter at Evergreen, I tried to register for the classes I wanted for my second quarter but was unable to get any of them. However, Evergreen has a program called Independent Learning Contracts. With an ILC, you, as the student, get to write a contract giving the terms of what and how you intend to learn. Once the contract is written, a faculty member must sponsor your learning contract. It really opens up an entire world of possibility for the student that cannot be found elsewhere. So, I wrote a contract and contacted every faculty member at the school. Most of the faculty members had no idea who I was, and every one of them told me they could not sponsor me. However, one teacher told me he had some open seats in his class. If I took this class, I would have the opportunity to go to Vietnam and China at the end of the quarter. I jumped so fast that I didn't have time to think it through. There was no "oh, how am I going to pay for this?" or any thoughts other than "I'm going to Vietnam and China!"

By the end of that quarter, I found myself sitting in a coffee shop in Hanoi, Vietnam, sampling the most expensive coffee in the world. I fell in love that day, and the course of my life would forever change. A week later I was studying tea in Wuyishan China for a week, and developing a love for tea as well. After that quarter, I began working on independent learning contracts through Evergreen that would turn me into an expert in the coffee industry.

Chapter 2

The Beginning of the Journey

While studying business at Centralia College, I began spending more and more time doing homework at coffee shops. It was easy for me to sit there and observe the day-to-day business of the companies, especially at Brownstone Coffee where my roommate was one of the baristas.

Brownstone was a really nice place with good coffee drinks, decent sandwiches made to order, a wine bar, a billiards table, a small stage for the weekly open mic night, and a really comfortable environment with leather furniture, and nice tables. They served Batdorf & Bronson's *Dancing Goats Blend* as their espresso bean. (Batdorf & Bronson is a coffee roasting company located in Olympia, Washington.)

In the beginning I gravitated towards the open mic night, as most of the last 15 years of my life had revolved around the music industry. However, as time went on, I began to notice signs of how not to run a coffee shop. For instance, many of the baristas didn't always charge their friends for their drinks. They were also always gossiping about each other behind the scenes, which led to poor attitudes toward the customers. A manager, who claimed to be the owner, was rarely on site unless he was showing up to embezzle money from the cash register to fuel his cocaine habit. They also allowed the store to frequently run out of necessities for the shop's daily orders. Needless to say, all this was a recipe for failure in any business.

It didn't take long before that manager was fired, and the actual owners brought in a kid fresh out of Gonzaga University to run the show. He showed up, guns blazing, quickly made some changes and figured out where the company was hemorrhaging.

He even asked me questions because he knew I had been observing the business the whole time. He built a plan to seal up the leaks and took action to mend them. Nearly everything changed behind the scenes, but the overall feeling of the place stayed inviting and comfortable. Within a couple of months the store bounced back and started thriving again.

The company was doing well, more business was coming through the doors, and there was a new acoustic music scene budding in the area. That is until the Christian rappers began to take over. Then it began to have the feeling of a Bible Study group. The clientele was changing, the other musicians were not showing up as often, and sales began to drop again. Then the manager's mother was diagnosed with ALS, and his head was no longer in the business. The company quickly started to tank again.. As a result, the owners decided to just get out and sell it. I was also in the process of transferring to The Evergreen State College. When this happened, I found a different coffee shop where I could study.

The coffee shop I began frequenting is a small craft roaster named Santa Lucia Coffee Roasters. They specialize in Arabica from Guatemala. Their owner, Justin Page, went down to the farms in Guatemala to help out a bit and see what goes into serving a cup of coffee in his shop. This was something that inspired me, although I hadn't yet realized where my passions lay.

However, I had also been traveling down a path of spirituality that was drawing me towards becoming a public speaker. I hadn't yet even found out that a trip to Vietnam and China was possible in my life, less, that I would be leaving on a class trip to Southeast Asia, but my roommate and I had begun thinking a coffee shop was a good business to start.

Yet, I was focused on heading towards a speaking career. I found that TEDx-Rainier (An event where the organizers get a group of speakers with unique ideas and gifts to the world and give them each 20 minutes to present to the audience) was taking place in Seattle, so I got a ticket to the event.

The one speaker I remember the most from the TEDx Rainier event was David Schomer who is touted as the person who brought the art of espresso to Seattle. He is the founder of Cafe Vivace which was just a small cart that he opened in 1988. During his talk, he spoke about his childhood introduction to the aroma of freshly ground coffee at the grocery store, and how when he finally tried coffee for the first time, he felt the disappointment that that aroma didn't translate into the cup. That experience took him on a lifelong journey to figure out how to successfully put that aroma into the freshly brewed drink. He talked about the engineering involved and the scientific studies he conducted to find that the best coffee shot is pulled between

24-26 seconds at 203°F with a temperature fluctuation of no more than a half of a degree during the being process.

David Schomer's talk was very interesting; I, of course, knew about Howard Shultz, the founder of Starbucks, but I had never really thought about the other true pioneers of the coffee industry until that day.

Continuing my coffee education, when I got back from my class trip to Vietnam and China, I always made sure to be at Santa Lucia during the times when Abram or Justin were roasting coffee, so I could watch and learn as much as I could. Then the idea to start a coffee roastery came to the forefront of my existence. During my travels I had learned about Kopi Luwak, and the Southeast Asian palm civets that produce it, and the horrible lives the farmers force these animals to live. This is how I could help them to live better lives: I would open a coffee roastery and espresso shop and sell Vietnamese coffee!

When I got home from that trip, I purchased a 20 foot long toy trailer that had been converted into an espresso shop. Sadly, as we moved it from where I bought it from, everything went crashing down. It was a very heartbreaking day to have the 'get up and go get em' dreams going full bore only to crash while losing $20,000 all on the same day. But, lesson learned. What I didn't know at the time was that would end up changing my course, as well.

During the quarter after the trip, I found a Vietnamese coffee wholesaler online, and I made the connection. Before long he sent me three 2kg samples: a Red Caturra Arabica, a Robusta, and a Robusta Peaberry. I took the samples to Santa Lucia and asked if I could roast them there. Justin was kind enough to allow me to do so. We roasted the samples and a few days later we cupped them and decided that the Red Caturra was going to be our main bean. It tasted good as espresso, in a latte, and as a pour-over. It even shined as drip coffee. The Robusta was bitter and just didn't taste very good. The Peaberry was quite a bit better, but it still didn't shine the way the Caturra did.

So, I knew what coffee I wanted to sell, but at this point, I didn't feel I knew enough about coffee to sell it properly. I went to school and asked my professor, Thuy Vu, if he would sponsor an independent learning contract for me. He agreed to do so and I wrote it up. The contract was for the summer quarter and I was to travel to Maui and Kona, Hawaii and study the coffee industry. I needed to see how and where it grows, and to understand what goes into the production of a cup of coffee.

Chapter 3
Hawaiian Coffee Adventure

For my first Independent Learning Contract, I traveled to Hawaii on a mission to study what goes into producing a cup of coffee, from sprouted seed to cup. My first lesson came on Maui where I learned about the dangers and destruction for which a tiny little beetle can be responsible. This lesson not only bored its way into my head through disappointment, but also an entire week into my adventure. I still hadn't seen a coffee plant; although I had sampled some amazing coffees. Next, I made my way to Kona, where my friend picked me up from the airport and took me to the property that he lives on. Along the way to his place we passed about 20 coffee plantations including the world famous Greenwell Estate and the Mountain Thunder Coffee Plantation.

As soon as we pulled into his driveway, I laid my eyes on the first coffee tree I have ever seen. Unfortunately, it was just before sunset and the cover from the macadamia nut trees, banana plants, and lilikoi vines blocked out most of the remaining sunlight. From what I could tell, the average coffee plant stood around eight to ten feet tall, with branches covered in small, unripened green coffee cherries.

The next morning my buddy drove me to pick up my rental car. Once that achievement was "unlocked" (I apologize for the video game reference because I don't even play!) I made my way up to the Mountain Thunder Plantation Cloud Estate. This farm is the highest elevation coffee plantation on the planet. I went on their short half-hour tour of their facilities. It began with samples of two of their coffee blends, and three tea varieties. One of the teas was a coffee cherry tea, called cascara, and the other two were varieties that only grow on the big island of Hawaii.

While we were sampling the libations, they played a twelve-minute video of the TV show "Dirty Jobs with Mike Roe" from when he visited the plantation in 2006. He had gone on their entire celebrity service tour which included going down into the plantation, picking cherries, slouching them around in the wet mill, and raking them out to dry. These were things I was unable to see during my upcoming short, little tour.

The tour guide began by showing us a couple of coffee trees. She explained that they grow two different species; Coffea Arabica, and Coffea Typica (a hybrid endemic to Hawaii.) Up until this day, I believed that Peaberry coffee was a separate species. The tour guide quickly dismantled this belief as she explained that as the seed matures, it splits perfectly down the center forming two coffee beans. Though, when this doesn't happen, the seed doesn't break, so it keeps the shape of a pea, hence the name. An interesting fact about the peaberry is that it can come from the same plant as the regular coffee beans, but it has an entirely different flavor profile.

The guide took us over to some previously harvested cherries and began to tell us about the coffee borer beetle that has been demolishing the crops. Fortunately, Mountain Thunder had only lost 30% of their crops since 2010 when it hit. Other farms on the islands had lost up to twice that amount. She showed us what the cherries look like when the beetle attacks them, as well as some samples of healthy ripe coffee cherries. Then she cracked one open and showed us the seed shell or parchment. We could see how the seed had a coating of sugary slime called mucilage. Then, she cracked that open and showed us how beans have another protective layer called silver-skin. Finally, she peeled that chaff from the beans and revealed to us a couple of tiny olive green coffee beans, explaining this is the way they are supposed to look before drying.

After the lesson in cherry and bean health, she took us to the dry mill, which is the room where the seeds are processed: they are shelled in one machine. The silver skin is removed in the next instrument. Then the beans are sorted by grade in the next contraption. They are then sorted by weight on the following piece of equipment to remove any bad beans that made it through the wet milling process. The one thing that all the previous machines are unable to do is sort out is the bad colored beans. The final computer in the dry mill is a very special tool and the only one of its kind on the island. It inspects 100% of the coffee beans with a laser. It determines if the bean is the correct color. If the coloring is off, it shoots the bean with a gust of air and kicks it out of the batch.

There are five different grades that depend on size, moisture, and purity. The grading from best to worst goes as Kona Extra Fancy, Kona Fancy, Kona

Select, and Kona Prime, then the one we don't talk about because it gets used as compost.

From there, she took us into the roast-master classroom. They have a five-pound roaster for the students and a 20-pound craft roaster for custom orders. She then explained the roasting process and showed us the three different roasts that Mountain Thunder is famous for, American Roast, (light or cinnamon roast) Vienna Roast, (medium roast), and their French Roast (dark roast). This concluded my first coffee tour.

The second farm on my journey was called Hula Daddy Coffee Plantation. They have been in business for a couple of decades. Originally, when they purchased the land, it was all a bed of lava rock. The owners had to drill 7000 holes in the rock where they planted two-year-old trees. They got their first small harvest a year later. They didn't know what they were doing yet, so their coffee was not very good. Since then they hired cherry pickers who only pick the ripest cherries on the plantation, and they average 500-700 pounds of coffee cherries per day. With15 cherry pickers, it takes them three weeks to harvest the ripened cherries, starting from the bottom of the plantation and working their way up to the top. Once they get to the top, they go back to the bottom and start the process all over again.

On this farm I watched the pickers take their daily haul to the sorting table, where they sort the thousands of cherries by hand, discarding anything that has insect damage, or that may not be quite ripe enough. As I watched the sorting of the cherries, I noticed all kinds of little maggot-like creatures jumping all over the place. These creatures were the larvae of the coffee borer beetle.

After the cherries get hand sorted, they take the cherries to the wet mill, where they sift out the rest of the deficient cherries by putting them in a vat of water and removing any of the fruits that float. Once this step is completed, they begin the processing. First, they remove the skin from the cherries. Once this process is taken care of, they take the beans that are still in their "underwear." covered in a protective parchment and the sticky, sugary film of mucilage that covers the parchment. They leave the seeds in a tub of water and allow it to ferment for about 24 hours. This process removes the mucilage from the parchment. Once this has taken place, they rake them out on large drying beds, where they leave them for three days or until they get to about 11% moisture.

When the beans are dry, they dump them in a machine that removes the parchment. Then they are sucked into another piece of equipment that gets rid of the silverskin. Once the parchment and silverskin is removed, they send the waste to become compost. The shelled beans are then sifted with a grading machine similar to that at Mountain Thun-

der. Then they roast the beans to order. Unfortunately, when I arrived at this farm they were out of
coffee, and they were just beginning to be able to
pick the cherries again.

I went to a couple of other farms on my third day in
Kona, but most of them had basically the same
things to show and tell. However, I also visited
Kona Joe's Coffee Company and this place is truly
unique in the way they do things. They even have
the patent to prove it.

The owner of Kona Joe's is an orthopedic surgeon
from the Californian wine country. He had the idea
of growing the coffee trees the same way the wine
grape growers grow their grapes by tying the
branches to trellises, and teaching the plants to naturally grow horizontally instead of vertically. This
method of growing has so many benefits in the
production of the coffee cherries as opposed to traditional methods. The most noticeable benefit is

that the plants each yield 30% more cherries than the standard way of growing the trees. Since they grow horizontally, they catch much more of the sun rays, which causes them to grow larger and ripen faster. Another happy accident that came from this method is the fact that the coffee is naturally less acidic.

I paid 15 dollars for their short tour, accompanied with a cup of coffee, and a coffee cup to take home as a souvenir. At the end of the trek, I asked if they sold green coffee, and shipped it to the states. They told me that they do sell green beans from other farms but not their own. I continued the conversation and gave them some of my knowledge that they were unaware. I explained that white coffee is getting popular in Washington State. They had never heard of a white roast before, so I explained how when cooking a white roast the beans had to release from the roaster at 330 degrees which occurs well before the first crack. Of course, this roast is extremely acidic because the acids and oils haven't baked out of the beans, and the caffeine content is extremely high. Bruno, the manager of the farm, had never even heard of white coffee, and he was very intrigued. He gave me his business card and told me we would work something out; however, it would probably cost about $2000 for a 100-pound bag of beans. I gave him a little box of Chehalis Mint candies and my business card. He was quite surprised and told me that he enjoyed the way I do business. He then went on to say that he is getting ready to start his distributorship of Kona Coffee from the small farms of the area. I was pretty sure I found a connection I was looking for, here in Hawaii.

Next I headed to Greenwell Farms, the last farm that I knew I needed tour. Greenwell is the largest coffee company in Kona. The Greenwell family has been, up until recently, ranching cattle in Kona since the last queen of Hawaii, Queen Liliuokalani, sold 35,000 acres of land to Henry Greenwell in 1850. They have also been cultivating coffee for 135 years. The current president of the company is Thomas Greenwell who is the fourth generation to run the family business.

I took the free tour of the farm which was the only farm I had been to that was already in full running capacity. The tour guide showed us the first trees that were planted on the plantation 135 years earlier. After that, she showed us some trees that were in their prime (20 years old) where we learned about how they prune one-third of their crop every year, leaving two-thirds in production every season.

She took us over to the drying trays which are huge floors with manually retractable roofing. These floors had been covered in layers of coffee beans that were drying in the sun, and a guy was walking through them with a rake every half an hour to ensure even drying of the beans.

She took us up to the open-air gift shop and tasting area, where they had ten different varieties of coffee to sample. I sampled a few, as I sparked up a conversation with the tour guide. When I told her about my mission, she said to "head down to the office and ask for Tommy." I followed her instructions.

41

I made my way down to the Greenwell Farms office. A receptionist greeted me, "How may I help you?" I replied, "I was told to come down here and ask to speak to Tommy because I am studying the coffee industry." I replied. "Let me go see if he is still here. He may have left for lunch already. I'll be right back." The receptionist got up and left out the back door, returning a couple of minutes later, "He will meet you outside at the picnic table shortly." She informed me while pointing out the door that I had entered. I thanked her graciously then walked outside.

Just as I walked outside, an older man walked up to me and extended his hand towards me for a handshake, "Thomas Greenwell President and CEO of Greenwell Farms, pleased to meet you." I took his hand and introduced myself and told him about my independent learning contract. We sat down at the table, and he started telling me about how his great-great-great-grandparents had bought the land from the queen of Hawaii. A little into this story, I thought I should be recording this, so I pulled my phone out and asked him if it was okay if I recorded the conversation. When I told him it would help me write my paper for school, he agreed.

Thomas: There's great coffees grown around the world, no doubt. What I have found is you have ten different farmers, you can have ten different coffee flavors from the same variety of tree grown in the same microclimate, next to each other.

It's not just where that coffee is grown, it's, obviously growing coffee is very Important, that step of it -- that you have the right varietal, for the right microclimate, and you have the right growing techniques; keep it all simple.

Then, processing, picking. Processing -- how you process, fermentation, and mucilization, dry fermentation, naturals. That's just – bang!

I ferment mine overnight in 12 hours; another farmer does it in 14, another one does it in 18. Which one's the best? I don't know. But it will be different.

I always say -- cleanliness is next to the best cup of coffee.

All the way through, from the farming right through processing. Then of course, after that -- not

43

unlike a bottle of wine, if we keep that, If we are each given a bottle of wine out of the same barrel, and we both take care of that bottle of wine properly, and you open up your bottle of wine today, and I open up my bottle of wine two months later, the winemaker will come in expect it to taste the way you put it in that bottle, know that.

With coffee, we roast it, package it that day, and you take yours home and make it with your coffeemaker and your water and all that, and I take it home and make it with my coffeemaker and my water, or side by side, again, you're going to have two different cups of coffee. Just the difference in the water. Be all filtered water, but some water can be with a lot of solids in it, undissolved solids. Other water can be so clean. You would think that would be the best water, but it's actually not the best water.

I guess the best book to write would be "There's 1001 ways to ruin a good cup of coffee," he laughed.
I guess it's easy in the coffee industry to be different. We each pick up our way of...

In very few places in the world do they take the coffee from the seed, from the nursery, right to the retail. We're one of the few in the world.

We tend to build to control what we -- just about everything but the weather.

Varietals. Varietals are probably the biggest major distinction I would say in a flavor of coffee from the same region. I believe in playing with varietals so that I can have more than one product.

Talked to someone the other day -- you ever go into a store, and they only sell one product?

They have traces so that they can get more people in their store, more people buying different things, and I think the only way you can really do that on a single farm like this -- you could do some naturals, some honey dry, different ways -- and you can come up with different products. But the varietals probably will impart the biggest difference at the farming level.

That's pretty simple.

Tony: Would you say that if you were to grow multiple different varieties of plants, like -- I know you guys have vanilla and cacao on the farm here -- if you were to cultivate that closer in with the coffee trees, do you think you might find some of the hints of that in the flavors or anything like that?

Thomas: No. Because, let's say, a mango –
 when you think of mango taste, it's in that fruit. The roots of that tree isn't giving off a mango taste. A mango falls on the ground is a rotten mango. That's not really a good taste. It wouldn't represent. I disagree.

We actually went through a few of those because there are copies of coffees and Hawaii tea so was it my tea? Or, I forget now, what... What?
This came out of my field. I don't have anything else but coffee out there.

But those are just different nuances beans produce. What produces chocolate-tasting coffee? It has a lot of chocolate in it. Not because it's growing around chocolate or cacao. Cacao tastes nothing like chocolate in their flavor.

It's different properties of the soil that may impart our coffee to taste a little bit more on the chocolate notes.

Processing. I can take coffee, scrub all the mucilage off of it, rinse it in water, dry it in 24 hours, and what do I have? I have a very mild cup of coffee.

Or I take this coffee, process it, ferment it overnight, wash it real clean, dry it, and that same coffee will have — more acidity, more balanced body, a little more body, because of the chemical changes that happen during fermentation.

You dry coffee with the mucilage on it. You'll get a sweeter coffee because it absorbs into the bean. So you get this little bit sweeter tasting coffee.

You dry it in the skins, and you get a heavy, heavy fruitiness from the coffee pulp, the skin, almost to the point of being over-fermented. Think about it -- it's fermenting in the bean, basically, in that cherry until it's dry.

There's a confusion a lot of times between over-fermentation and fruitiness. Sourness. Sourness is very closely related to fruitiness, and it's a fine line.

47

When I first learned how to cup coffee, and we were in this workshop, and we were tasting, I never really tasted sourness; I've smelled it, but not tasted it. Oh, this coffee is really fruity -- it was sour.

So even our Department of AG over here, that certifies our coffee, you take naturals... You know what a natural is? That's coffee dried to the skin -- and they will fail it for sourness. They are only looking for defects; they're not looking for attributes, so we've got to retrain them, and they get confused, so that...

Unlike other products, growing it next to other trees, don't really impart the taste, in my opinion; I have not been convinced. I don't know anyone that's tried to say really it has. I'm sure there's something that tree might give off that might change some flavor in the coffee, maybe. But I don't know.

Tony: What comes to mind when somebody asks what is success?

Thomas: What is success?

To me, success is, in the coffee business, at a farmer's level is growing coffee, producing a high volume of crop, picking it, being able to sell it for a sustainable price that carries the company forward into the next year; you've got to have a profit.

Whichever level you are at, that's success. I don't know that anybody that you've ever met that totally failed and gone bankrupt and said that they had a bit of success.

There's the sustainability. "Sustainability" is a very over-used word. Because if the government pays a payroll and you want everybody not to destroy the forest and not to cause any erosion or not to cause impact on the land -- well there's not going to be any sustainability on that land other than the plants growing.

Because even all the way back -- you take Hawaii, when the Hawaiians lived here, sustainability was for them to be able to feed themselves. They basically killed off half the native birds on the island because there was nothing to eat here when they got here. Their protein source. It is easier to catch birds than fish. Making fishhooks out of bone was probably a 10% success rate of catching fish with it.

There are all kinds of neat stories out there. But a number of fishhooks we found were -- Wow! That's a lot of fishhooks in the bottom of the ocean. They tried a lot; if they caught a fish on it, the fishhook wouldn't be at the bottom of the ocean, right?

Success. Here's a success story -- right there. First place, this year. We got a variety called Pacamara, and that's a variety no one else is growing in Hawaii. I brought it in; we grew it; it took me three years to get to first place. Last year I was second place. Or not "me" but the farms. That's success. Now, does it do me any good winning first place if I can't sell the coffee? No. I gotta get people excited about it.

Tony: How do you do your marketing? What's your main focal point?

Thomas: For our retail, our roasted product, we market right here. You were there the other day. That was our first marketing point, and then it was people that came by the farm, they had a good time, they learned something about coffee they knew nothing about. We'd be surprised, you knowing more about coffee than the average person knows. The tour is maybe kind of... maybe not a whole lot.

Tony: It's short but informative.

Thomas: Yes. But it is short, because for a free tour

Tony: Exactly. Exactly.

Thomas: But it's enough for the person that's only known coffee to come from the gourmet store down the road or in a bag off the grocery store or some of these people still drink canned coffee.

When we first started... I'll tell you a little story. My father passed away in 92, and I took over management, and I was sitting in this chair   wondering what the hell am I going to do doing this?

I'm actually a diesel engineer, by heart and by... That's what I went to college for, and I came home early; never got a degree or anything. But I was good at it. But anyway.

So here I am, a coffee farmer. Was never my plan in my life, but I took it on because it was a family business and it was important that it kept going.

We used the land to produce cash for the family, and coffee seemed a good thing to do on a small amount of land.

So a car drives in, the guy goes -- what is this place? -- Out of the blue just drove in accidentally. And I was, "It's a coffee farm." And he goes --oh, do you sell coffee?

I go, now I got a customer; this is cool. "Yeah I do." -- How much? -- "Ten dollars a pound." -- Ten dollars? -- starts rolling up the window -- "Nobody in their right mind will pay that.

And I go, "I hope somebody does. Because I need it; I need ten bucks man."

He looks over, and he sees my processing facility. He looks -- oh, what's that out there on path? -- "That's coffee." He goes -- well why isn't it brown? -- "Because it's not roasted."

I go, "hey you got a few minutes? I've got to go over there and break coffee. I'll go show you what we're doing."

He goes -- No, no, that's OK. You're going to expect me to buy a pound of coffee after that.

I go, "I'll make you a deal. You come with me and I promise I won't even let you buy one if you beg me for a pound."

So he and his wife and two kids get out and we walk over and I talked to them about coffee; they're asking questions; I'm answering them. We get up; I show them the process that we go through. Up there raking.

Pretty soon they're up there raking all my coffee for me, taking pictures of each other.

There was the story about this. We're all done, and we're walking back and he goes -- you know, I feel very embarrassed now.

"Why? Don't feel embarrassed. I'm not going to charge you for the tour."

He goes -- no. You're not selling your coffee for enough money. After all that work for farming and picking and processing and then you got to let it rest for a month and a half, and then you got to mill it and then you got to roast it. That costs a lot of money to do all that.

I go, "that's what I think, but people like you obviously think I'm ripping you off."

He goes -- no, this is . . . Can I try some.

"Sure. I got a pot on my table in there. It's a couple of hours old, but you can help yourself."

So we go in and pour a couple of cups, and he says to his wife -- wow, this is the best cup of coffee I've ever had.

"It's two hours old, and it costs ten bucks a pound."

He looks up, and I have a few packages. Because I wasn't retailing, I was selling them in four-finger baggies.

He goes -- is that for sale?

I say "Yeah. But not to you."

He goes -- why?

I said, "I told you, I'm not going to let you buy a pound."

He goes -- how about five pounds?

I go, "that I can sell you."

And that was my first sale.

So that's what drove that. We just have a miller business that's probably bigger than our retail business, and that's because of people that come to the farm. And since they can't come back to Kona all the time, they come back on the Internet. We don't do any wholesale of the roasted product. We do have a product that we sell out. Our biggest business is shipping green coffee to roasters around the world. And a lot of them will use our name because it means something out there in the Kona coffee industry. Quality, number one. Because you're not going to find a bag of our coffee, that has crap in it. It does have my name on it. So we think that's what keeps it going, the quality.

I used to give tours to national farm bureau members. Most of them were retired, old farmers. They take a trip to Hawaii, so they come here, and we'd feed them some cookies and milk and coffee and fruit. I thought, "wow, right now I can give them a real tour to some farmers."

But, right over their head -- because it takes the time to understand an industry, whether it's coffee, corn, wheat, almonds, whatever.

So we learned really well just to keep the tour very simple. And history - everybody likes to know history. So we try to mix it up with a lot of different things and keep it interesting. But I think it works; it needs to be changed. Change doesn't come fast in Hawaii. Very slow.

That's basically the history in a nutshell.

I thanked him and gave him the gift of Chehalis Mint candies, and told him their significance. He was interested to know where Chehalis was located to get more of a feel of from where I was traveling. I also gave him my business cards and told him that I was in the process of starting up a coffee roastery. Thomas said that he loves startup companies, and he would do anything he could to help me in my ventures, even if it meant selling me a quarter of a bag at a time to get me started. I asked him prices, and he gave me a firm quote. I thanked him again and told him I was very grateful that he had taken the time to talk to me, then we parted ways.

On my final visit to a coffee plantation in Kona, I went back to Mountain Thunder's Cloud Forest Estate, the highest altitude coffee farm in the world. On this visit, I was there to learn how to roast the beans so they would be ready for cupping. The best part was I would be taking the batch of coffee that I would roast home with me.

I showed up early for my reservation, so I went on the free tour once again. This time, the tour was led by a different person, but it was pretty much the same, maybe a little less informative. I think the tour guide had very brief experience on the farm. I did learn a few new things. The cherry pickers get paid by the bean and average around $65.00 per 100-pound sack of cherries, and the good pickers average 7-8 sacks per day. I also learned that I could come back the next season. Or stay for this season and do their WWOOFing program (World Wide Opportunities of Organic Farming), where I would get the chance to pick the cherries, run them through the wet mill, and send them through the dry mill, for a couple of months.

At the end of the tour, I met up with the farm's Roast-master, Michael. We exchanged pleasantries, and I found out that he is originally from Portland. He was excited that I was actually there to learn instead of being the run-of-the-mill tourist.

He took me into the roasting room that had a five-pound drum roaster, and a 35-pound drum roaster made by Dietrich. In between the two machines was a floor scale with a bucket filled with five pounds of green coffee beans.

I flipped the switch to ignite the natural gas flame on the five-pound machine, and we had to wait about 10 minutes for the drum to heat up to 400 degrees Fahrenheit. I picked up the bucket and dumped it into the funnel at the top of the machine then pulled a lever and the beans poured into the drum. I noticed that when I added the beans, the temperature dropped down to 180 degrees. Once the beans were officially roasting, I watched as the temperature slowly rose back up.

On the front of the machine there is a round tub, hooked to a fan for cooling the beans after they get roasted, so they quickly stop cooking. There is also a handle that is a spoon that takes samples of the coffee directly from the drum that is used to monitor the color of the roast. It is imperative to keep a very close eye on the roast because merely a few seconds difference can ruin an entire batch of coffee. If one were to ruin a 35-pound batch, they basically threw away $5000.00 of finished product.

When the temperature reached 375 degrees, I noticed that the color was starting to darken. I reached over and increased the airflow into the drum by a notch, which also added more room inside the drum for the beans to expand. I was waiting to hear the beans start to imitate the sound of wet Rice Krispies "Snap, Crackle, Pop!" what is known as "first-crack" the point where the oils of the bean are first beginning to release. My roast reached this point at 400 degrees. I checked the coloration of my roast, and it was still a bit lighter than I wanted. I reached over and turned up the airflow another notch; then I let the roast go about another 45 seconds. I checked the color again at 412 degrees, and it was perfect. I reached over and switched the airflow over to the cooling fan and pulled the lever allowing the roasted beans to barrel out into the cooling tray. I had to stir the beans manually for four minutes as they cooled down to room temperature.

Once the beans were cooled, I poured them into a bucket again and took them to the next room where I was given 17 coffee bags equipped with gas release nozzles and 17 Vienna Roast stickers to apply to them. I placed the labels on the bags and dumped the beans into the hopper of the bag filling machine. My guide set the machine to weigh in four-ounce increments. I sat down in front of the gadget and placed the first bag over the bag filling chute. The machine dumped four ounces of my beans into the top of the chute, and I stepped on a button that opened the door of the chute, and the bag filled with coffee. I repeated this until all 17 bags had been filled.

Then I took the filled bags to the sealing machine, where I placed four bags at a time onto the gadget that has a large nitrogen tank standing next to it.

After I had gotten the bags in place, I pushed a button, and the machine shot nitrogen into the bags and then sealed them. The process was then over.

I had decided that my coffee roasting experience was going to be my last trip to a coffee farm on this voyage. When I woke up on my last day there, my friend went to work, and I jumped in the car. I didn't have a plan. I figured I would just go where the day would take me.

About a half a mile away from my friend's driveway, I saw a sign that I hadn't noticed before, though I must have driven past it 50 times while I was there. The sign showed a happy Buddha drinking a cup of coffee, and it said, "Buddha's Cup Coffee Estate next right." Seeing how the logo for my roastery idea was a Buddha, I had to go check this farm out. I followed the directions which took me on a three-mile sign chasing tour that finally led me to a dirt road with another Buddha's Cup sign and a no trespassing sign. I ignored the sign and drove on the dirt road for another mile and a half until I found the coffee farm. There was a big sign that said "Closed for remodeling" that I noticed when I pulled up.

The farm manager came out of the office with a perplexed, confused, and interested look on her face. I got out of the car and engaged her. I told her about my contract, and she was very welcoming. I followed her into the office, and she asked me what my favorite roast was. I told her medium, and she brewed a pot of French press coffee. We sat down and drank it, and she explained to me about the farm which was actually five plantations, and each one was a different brand. But the Buddha's Cup was special because all the coffee that goes into a Buddha's Cup bag has been grown under a sacred tree.

I just so happened to have a final box of mints, so I gave it to her and told her about them, as well as my businesses I have been cultivating. She was very impressed and said that she nearly bought a house in Chehalis. She asked me if I wanted to take a tour of the farm, so I enthusiastically agreed. The processing part of the farm was getting remodeled, so I wasn't able to see any action, but she showed me how they grew the coffee trees under these sacred trees. She also showed me the five different varieties of tea they were growing including two that only grow at very high altitude on the big Island of Hawaii. She showed me their three Rainbow Eucalyptus trees, which was exciting because I had really wanted to see the Rainbow Forest on Maui, but I couldn't find it. Then she showed me where the wet mill was getting built, as well as the drying decks, the dry mill, and the roasting room. Then she took me back to the office and showed me what they had for sale. I purchased a half-pound bag of coffee from her and asked about their burlap tote bags they had for sale. She said, "Usually, we sell them for 35 dollars, but I want to give one to you as a gift." Then I asked about green coffee. She said how much do you need? A pound? Five tons? We can help you with whatever your needs are."

I departed and went back to letting the day take me where it would. I then drove toward the airport to get gas at Costco. Along the drive, there lays a national park that looks like an ancient lava flow and is very desolate. I had driven past it too, many times since I had been there. This time, I heard a whisper that told me to stop and check it out. I got out of my car and found a sign that had a map on it of a mile hike over to an ancient fish trap. I thought that might be kind of interesting. So I headed that way. When I got there, I first saw a grass hut like what the ancient Hawaiians would have lived in. Then I saw a huge bay with a stone structure out in the center of it and noticed that the water was no deeper than thigh-high. . It was cool, but it got much more awesome the longer I was there. Soon I noticed these little round things floating in the water. I took a closer look and found myself surrounded by hundreds of green sea turtles! It was a very surreal moment. I spent a good portion of the day with these magnificent creatures. Then I headed back to the car and finished my trip to the gas station.

Once I filled up, I drove back to my friend's house. When I pulled into his driveway, I noticed that he had loaded his kayak into the bed of his truck. I got out of the car, and he asked me if I was about ready to go for an adventure? I said, "I'm game, let's go!" So we got into his truck. He drove back the way I had come, and then turned onto King Kamehameha III Drive, which took us to the Sheraton Resort. This is the only location where you can eat dinner and watch the manta rays while they feed.

We headed inside the hotel and over to the observation deck, where we watched the sunset. There were already five boats hanging out a couple of hundred yards off of the shore. Once the sun had gone to bed for the night, we went back out to the truck and drove over to where we could put my friend's kayak into the water. After we got the boat unloaded, we hopped on it and paddled out to where the boats were. When we arrived, we found about 200 people holding onto six floating devices with bright lights shining down into the water.

I put on my mask and snorkel, affixed my dive light to my wrist, then I rolled out of the boat into the water. At first, all I could see were a few needlefish, and the water was about 20 feet deep. Up until this point in my life, I had never been in open water this deep or this far away from a shoreline. I must admit, I was a little bit anxious. After a few minutes went by, it happened. I laid my eyes on my very first real live wild manta ray! It was just a baby, but it was still a good seven feet from wing tip to wing tip. I was in complete awe if this little gentle giant. The next thing I knew there were eight of them gliding around me in the water, doing their gracious barrel rolls that they are known for while they feed. One of these beautiful fish was easily 15 feet across. I recognized him from the pictures inside the hotel because its left facial appendage was deformed, so they had named it Lefty.

These amazing creatures were heavily attracted to the lights from the tour, and they were frequently swimming up and rubbing their bellies on the snorkelers who had paid to be in the water. It was probably the most exciting thing I have ever witnessed in my life. I had completely forgotten about my anxiety, or even where I was at the moment. All I could focus on was how amazing these giants are, and that I was right next to them.

About 20 minutes into their feeding frenzy, Lefty came over and checked me out very intimately. At one point his beautifully deformed face was literally less than a foot away from my face. I could see inside his gills that he uses to filter the plankton from the water. It was a life-changing instant. Around ten minutes later, the Rays swam off into the abyss. The tourists climbed back into their tour boats, and I pulled myself back into the kayak, and we all headed back to the shore.

I know that a few of these experiences don't tie into what I learned about the coffee industry; however, they did remind me of why I chose the coffee industry in the first place. I believe that when one's "why" is strong enough, there is nothing that can stand in the way of one's success. I chose the coffee industry after I tasted Kopi Luwak, or what they call weasel coffee in Vietnam. After I had found that amazing brew, I found out how terribly those de-valued animals get treated. So, I decided that I could eventually help them by using coffee to raise money to help the Kopi Luwak farmers turn their coffee farms into giant cages that are also permaculture farms, where the animals can live as they would in the wild (after they have been litter box trained, of course.) I know that at $800 a pound, I wouldn't be able to stop anyone from producing it.

After these experiences, I became interested in broadening my charitable efforts to help endangered species in the areas where I source my products. I want to use proceeds from Kona coffee to help the populations and protections of the giant green sea turtles, and the giant manta rays. I want to use Thai coffees to help the tigers and the elephants. This is the steadfast backbone of my perseverance.

Chapter 4
Locating Coffee in Thailand

My second coffee-related Independent Learning
Contract was to Thailand and Vietnam to see some
of the differences in how the products are produced
in their cultures as opposed to in Hawaii as well as
to meet my coffee supplier face to face and make
some other connections along the way.

About two months after I returned from my trip to
Hawaii, I left on a journey that would span a month
and a half. I flew out of LAX in Los Angeles to
Shanghai, China where I nearly missed a connecting flight to Kunming, China where I caught my
connecting flight to Chiang Mai, Thailand. I arrived
late at night, rented my car and went to my hotel.
After I was checked in, I checked into the bed. It
had been a very long day.

In the morning my first instinct was to head over to
the Jade Buddha Temple, where I was able to pur-

chase a jade elephant and a couple of jade hearts. I could have purchased a replica of the Buddha, but sadly taking Buddha out of the country of Thailand is illegal, and I'd already dealt with customs agents too much on this trip. I would love to have one, though. Happily, for me, the monk offered to let me take a photo of the real thing.

When I left the temple my next stop was the breakfast place I wanted to visit, named Libernard Cafe. The owner of the shop brought me a menu. I ordered an Americano, a banana pancake (the house specialty), and two fried eggs. When she brought me the coffee, I took a sip and it was nearly as good as the amazing coffee I had become a connoisseur of in Kona. When she brought me my food, I said: "The coffee is very good." She put her hands together and bowed her head with a smile and replied, "My family grows the coffee. Lonely Planet ranked us best coffee in Thailand. Would you like to buy some?" I answered with a big smile, "Let me

eat my breakfast, and then we can talk coffee."
While I was eating I looked them up and she was
telling the truth about being the best, not that my
taste buds had lied to me.

When I had finished my meal and I paid for my
food, I told her my reason for being in Thailand,
and that I was setting up a coffee import company. I
asked if she sold green coffee, and she answered
affirmatively. I gave her my business card and purchased 2 kilos of green coffee to sample roast when
I got home. I only paid 240฿ which equals to $.55
cents per pound. (What had I just stumbled into?)
She told me that her daughter would email me and
we could set something up. I thought I could get
220 pounds shipped for about $500, but my ship-
ping math might have been off at this point. Still, it
was very exciting!

I walked around for the rest of the day looking for a
hat while stopping at any temple I stumbled across.

I am amazed at the shortage of hats in Chiang Mai. I finally headed back to Warorot Market, where I finally found said hat. Then I located some food and went back to my room.

I had been dallying around mostly doing the tourist thing, waiting for my friend Gretchen (who lives in Chiang Mai) and her co-worker Tim to get their days off so we could make the 3-hour drive up to Chiang Rai the coffee capital of Thailand.

For most of the last couple hundred years, Thailand had been one of the world's leading cultivators of opium poppy flowers. This lasted until King Ram IX Bhumibol Adulyadej, took power. He decided that he didn't want his country to be known for its drugs. Instead, he worked with the farmers to replace the opium fields with coffee. This move made it so the people truly loved the King. Sadly, he passed away a few days before I arrived in Thailand.

One of the biggest coffee companies in Thailand is named Doi Chaang Coffee. One of their two owners is a Canadian businessman; the other is a Thai National. This company was instrumental in helping the King achieve his goal of getting rid of the opium. Their largest farm is located away in the mountains near Chiang Rai, Thailand.

On the morning of my fifth day in Chiang Mai, I checked out of my hotel to go meet up with Gretchen and Tim. We had lunch, then loaded into the car, and began our journey to nearly the northern border of Myanmar and Laos, the area where most of the Thai coffee is grown.

Once we finally got out of the civilized area we found ourselves in the luscious green countryside. I have seen some beautiful mountains in my time, and these mountains are absolutely stunning. The highway had a lot of switchbacks, which made the drive time seem much shorter than it actually was.

An hour into our trek we stopped at Rabbit Crew Farm & Coffee, which was just a little pull off from the highway. The coffee shop was built of two shipping containers stacked on top of each other with a window and door cut into the side. Inside was a counter, and the tiniest espresso machine I had ever seen. The three of us ordered our drinks and checked out their farm while we drank them. During this stop, we found our first coffee plants from the trip. I showed them to Gretchen and Tim and explained a little bit about ripening. I showed them the difference between the ripe cherries that were optimal for harvesting, and the ones that were not quite ready, and the cherries that have already been tainted by the coffee beetle. Once we finished our drinks, we jumped back into the car hand headed back on our excursion.

When we arrived in Chiang Rai, it was getting kind of late in the afternoon. We got checked into our hostel and we quickly made a friend with a professional backpacker named Emma, who was born in New Zealand. She grew up in Australia, and currently, resides in Vancouver BC. We all decided it was time to go find a bite to eat for dinner. We walked around town for a little bit and through the night market. We were having all kinds of trouble finding a decent place to eat that catered to vegetarians. Finally, we found an Indian restaurant named Accha Fusion India. We had a smorgasbord of curry, masala, onion baji, pakora, and naan bread. The meal was fantastic. Later I found out that it was rated the number one Indian restaurant in Thailand.

In the morning, the four of us loaded into the car and headed out to the Doi Chaang Coffee Plantation. This visit was the entire reason for coming to Thailand. We thought it was only another 15-minute drive away from the temple but we were wrong. It ended up taking us an hour and fifteen minutes to get there. The road was extremely windy and riddled with switchbacks. The car I was driving was having problems with the steepness of the mountain. At one point there were cliffs on both sides of the road. It was a fun, yet, stressful drive.

When we got there, we could see a wet processing mill that was just beginning its work for the season. There was also a coffee and gift shop, and the Doi Chaang Coffee University. (I wish I had known about this when planning this trip because I think my plans would have changed up a bit.) We ordered cups of coffee and checked out the gift shop.

I found that they were selling wild civet coffee. This stuff was much more expensive than the stuff I had picked up in Vietnam where it was about $400 a pound, and was produced by caged animals that are not treated very well. Here at Doi Chaang, I picked up 50 grams for 1150฿ or $33.00 USD. They were also selling it for 300฿ per cup, or $8.50 US.

When I asked if they sold green coffee, I was given a business card and told I could contact the owner of the company whose office is located in Bangkok. This was fortunate considering I planned on arriving in Bangkok in a couple days.

Unfortunately, we were unable to find the actual Doi Chaang Coffee Farm. However, we were able to see a lot of coffee plants in different stages of their life cycle.

At the top of the mountain where we found ourselves, we could see coffee plants for as far as the eye could see.

Chapter 5
Meeting the Farmer of My Favorite Coffee

My first meeting with Lan from O'Lan Farms took a few days to accomplish after I flew into Dalat City. Not because our schedules were not matching up, but because, I was stricken with food poisoning. (When traveling around the world, especially for any prolonged amount of time, it's not unusual to run into this Our bodies just get used to the eating culture of where we spend most of our time, and eating street food can be a shock to the system.) I had eaten some vegan food from a street vendor when I got into town, and the next day was absolutely terrible. I'll spare you the details.

The following morning I messaged Lan and she gave me an address where I could meet up with her. I grabbed a taxi and went to pick her up outside of a university. Our 20-kilometer drive out to her family farm took about an hour, but along the way, I learned she was the head of a security firm in Dalat City, and that coffee farming was kind of the side gig. This seemed kind of crazy to me because her farm grows the best of the best Vietnamese Highland Arabica. As we drove up into the mountains, I began to see nothing but coffee and tea plantations everywhere, and the views were stunningly beautiful. This area is the place of postcard photo dreams.

When we finally arrived at the farm, we had to climb a very steep driveway up to the house. The concrete was slippery with moss that was textured similar to seaweed growing on it. Once we summited the driveway, we were greeted by a younger man in coveralls who was completely covered in mud. Lan introduced him as her brother, and I thought it would be great to get a photo with him. Next, Lan took me inside where she introduced me to her beautiful family: Father, Mother, her other brother, sister in law, and her toddler nephew. We sat down for a little while as we drank green tea together. The whole time there was an interesting experience because Lan and I were the only ones in the room who spoke any English. But her father was very interested in me, and I could tell that he is quite the everyday comedian. Everyone in the family was filled with so much joy and happiness, the kind of thing that most Americans would see and become jealous. However, it made me feel warm and welcomed.

After tea time, Lan and her brother (who I had just learned was also a police officer) took me out to gallivant through the farm to show me some of the different varietals of coffee they were growing. Their farm seemed gigantic: 20,000 acres of coffee, persimmons, mango, banana trees, and of course a vegetable garden. We spent a little time picking some of the coffee cherries. There wasn't a lot to pick because the harvest season was just in its beginning stages for the year. And I was "forced" to experience the fresh persimmons and mango right from the tree. It was a difficult thing to swallow. (Ha-ha, I would recommend it to anyone.) But beware, the persimmons are very tasty and flavorful fruit, but it dries your mouth out much faster than cranberries.

Lan was growing Red Caturra, Typica, and Catamor, which are all common specialty-grade Arabica species. She also grows a small plantation of Robusta, the most common species of coffee grown in Vietnam, but she also had something very special and rare. Lan grows one of the rarest strains of coffee in the world, a strain that I had no idea even existed until I got to the farm. This coffee is called Yellow Caturra. The coffee fruit is referred to as coffee cherries because they look like Bing cherries. When ripe they normally have a dark red skin on them and they look quite appetizing. When the Yellow Caturra cherry ripens its skin becomes this bright lemon yellow color crayon, every kid would use it to color in the sun on their drawings.

I'll tell you from experience, that Vietnamese Yellow Caturra is expensive, but roasted to a medium or Vienna roast, it is worth every penny you will pay for it.

While we were out in the coffee bush, Lan's mother prepared a vegetarian meal for us, including the taxi driver. Every ingredient she used was freshly picked from the garden and prepared while we were picking coffee.

After the meal, the entire family and I went outside to the front of the house and had our photos taken. I gave Lan and her mother each a box of the Chehalis Mints before saying goodbye to the family. We walked back down the treacherous driveway to the taxi and began driving back towards town Lan started to tell me more about the coffee industry of the area.

The specialty Arabica is grown in the highest part of the mountains there, about 1000 meters above sea level. The Robusta is grown below that, so there is much more Robusta grown in Vietnam than Arabica. O'Lan Farms are among the very few that hand picks every coffee cherry. From what I understood it was much like they do in Kona. Not only that, but they also sun dry and remove the skins and parchment by hand. It's a very labor intensive process. They are very proud to claim their coffee is the best in Vietnam because they do not use machines, so they do not get unripened beans in their harvests. This is exactly what I was hoping to hear. This care really shines through in a cup of the brewed java. It tastes like the coffee wants to taste in a competition. It's sweet, fruity, chocolaty, nutty, and everything you would expect from a world-class cup of coffee.

Most of the other coffee farms in Vietnam use machines to harvest their cherries. This leaves so much room for error. In a batch of coffee harvest like this, some cherries are perfect, but there also will be under-ripe and over-ripe beans as well. Having these in a batch of coffee causes the flavor to become pungent and bitter, sometimes even sour. Comparing a cup from O'Lan Farms and a cup from the average farm in Dalat, Vietnam is like comparing a high-end Mercedes to a Kia Rio. The Rio will get the job done, but you really enjoy driving the Mercedes. And, of course, you get what you pay for.

My stomach was still a bit off from the food poisoning, so we headed back to Lan's office in the city where she made a cup of artichoke tea for me to help settle my stomach, and some coffee of her personal blend. It was a good end to a perfect day with a new friend. We made plans to meet up the next day and go visit the weasel coffee farm and then parted ways. I took the taxi back to the hostel, and gave the taxi driver a box of the candies as a "thank you" along with a 250,000 Dong tip. It always warms the soul to see a face light up like that.

Chapter 6

Kopi Luwak...
The Best Shit You'll Ever Drink... Literally.
But it's Not Okay...
Though, it can be.

The next morning, Lan sent me an address where to meet her, so I left my hotel and grabbed another cab, to the Dalat railway station. She must have just ridden in from out by her family farm. We stopped so she could get a cup of coffee, and then headed out to the Trai Ham Dalat Weasel Coffee Farm which was about two kilometers away. They produce the world famous "cat poop" coffee.

It was in Indonesia where it was first discovered that this creature had a taste for the coffee fruit. When the Dutch first inhabited the Sumatra area, they planted vast jungles of coffee plants, and they wouldn't allow the locals to taste the beverage. One day, one of the Sumatrans noticed that the civet (a house-cat-sized, tree-dwelling weasel) had been eating the fruit of the coffee and was leaving behind the entire seeds of the coffee, undigested. So he collected the animal droppings and processed and roasted the beans, and the legend of Kopi Luwak was born. (History: In the wild, the palm civet only picks and eats the ripest coffee cherries, much like humans pick fruit for themselves.)

When we arrived, we were greeted politely and Lan asked if we could see the animals. There were two of them sleeping in cages on the counter next to a tray of beans that were drying after being washed. The farm storekeeper led us down to a shed that had probably 40 cages that were around 8 feet tall by 4 feet wide and 6 feet deep. Each cage had a box the weasel could hide in, a branch it could climb down to eat the ripened coffee cherries, and a ledge that is used as a litter box. The poor civets were so shy of people, yet they were so cute. I fell in love with the little things.

It broke my heart to see these poor animals so unhappy. Yet, at the same time, it validated one of my greatest ideas in how to change the Kopi Luwak industry. (I'll get back to that shortly.) Not only did I see proof that they are easily litter box trained, but I learned that they also get to eat bananas and other local fruits and veggies. That news made me feel a little better. I was told that each civet produces up to 10 kilograms of Kopi Luwak in a season, and they had 300 of them on the farm. They charge $1000 for a kilogram of their product. Apparently, the stuff I bought in Hanoi two years earlier was counterfeit at $17 for 350 grams.

After visiting the shed full of animals we headed back up to the bar, where I paid $5 a cup for Lan and myself. They brewed it in a vacuum siphon coffee brewing system, which consisted of two large glass bulbs; the bottom is filled with water and the top with the ground coffee. They are connected with a shaft that allows a vacuum pressure to lift boiling water up into the grounds. When removed from the heat it pours the freshly brewed and filtered coffee back down into the bottom bulb, then take them apart and serve the coffee. It was fun to watch, and it made for a great cup of coffee. Before we left, I purchased 20 grams for a dollar per gram. We were allowed to pet one of the Civets that was sleeping on the counter. Their fur is so soft, and it snuggled right up to the affection. Now I want to bring one home as my next dog. I did a little research and apparently, if you get them young, they make amazing pets with a personality that is crossed between a ferret and a dog. What a great friend that would be! The only real downfall is that if they do bite you, you would know it, because of their extremely sharp teeth. They smell like buttered popcorn all the time, and the odor gets stronger if they feel threatened.

The Animal

The palm civet is a mammal about the size of a large house cat. They are from the Viverrid family and are closely related to the weasel, ferret, and the mongoose. They are found to live in the tropical and logged forests all over Southeast Asia. Civets make wonderful pets if you can get over their rambunctious ferret-like personalities and their interesting popcorn-like odor. They have an average lifespan of around 15 years, and they love interacting with people if they are handled from an early age. They love to cuddle, have very soft fur, and aren't the type of critter that likes to destroy things. However, they are tree dwellers, so they naturally climb on everything and they have very sharp claws and teeth. They are easily litter box trainable. Their temperament and personality seem to be a cross between a dog and a cat. They get very excited if you grab a leash once they have figured out that it means they get to go for a stroll around the neighborhood. They are eager to learn and love to please their people. All this makes what I found during my research, and then I saw with my own eyes, so heartbreaking.

In November of 2016, I traveled to Dalat City, Vietnam, where I was able to visit a Kopi Luwak farm. I was able to convince one of the farmers to take me down to tour the living cages of the poor animals and explain to me their daily living conditions. It was very saddening to see that these very social animals, who need interaction with other creatures, were being kept in 8'x8'x4' cages with a small little wooden box with a hole in the side, a single plush toy, a litter box, and a bowl of coffee cherries, many of which were not up to fully ripened standards. I was told that the animals spend most of their lives in the cage, and all they get to eat is coffee cherries and a couple bananas per day.

They easily had 300 cages, and the civets that I saw, were very shy which is strange according to everything I had read and heard about them. This tells me that the farmers are unkind to the poor things. The tour guide took me back up to the sales hut, where they had a couple of civets, which were much more personable. I was allowed to play with them for a little bit. This is where I was able to experience how soft and cuddly and sweet they truly are. I paid 100,000 Dong (or $5 US) for a cup of the coffee and bought another 20 grams (about 4 cups worth) for another 400,000 Dong.

Since experiencing the civets' living conditions on this trip, I have been racking my brain on how I can help to make these creatures lives better, and I think I finally have a viable plan, though it is going to be a very expensive undertaking. However, I believe that my emergence into the coffee industry can spark a way to raise the money to make it happen.

My Plan

First things first; I needed to come up with a pitch
to give to the farmers that will make the effort seem
like it is worth their while. It needed to be something short with a lot of sales power. This is my ele-
vator pitch:

*The animals on this farm are very unhappy. They are
unable to interact with the other animals which they
need to do to be happy. The wild animals only eat the
best quality coffee cherries. They are very smart and easy
to train to use litter boxes. Happy cats will make happier
coffee than what is already being produced. Wild Kopi
Luwak gets 30% higher profit margins. Let's turn this
entire farm into a giant cage, train the animals to love
human contact and use litter boxes while they are young,
then put them into their wild environment inside the giant cage. Then they will eat only the best quality coffee
fruit and use the many litter boxes around the farm. The
animals will then be happier and so will the coffee.*

Implementation

Funding is going to be the most difficult part of this endeavor. I need to put together a not-for-profit organization that allows my customers to choose to round their order prices up in order to donate to the fund to build the farm sized cages and train the animals. I still need to research how much it will cost to transform the non-animal-friendly Kopi Luwak farms into animal-friendly farms. However, an educated guess says that it will probably cost right around $100,000 US per farm to make it happen. I am still unaware of how many different Kopi Luwak farms exist, but I believe there are less than 100. I do know that they exist in Indonesia, Vietnam, Thailand, Cambodia, Laos, and the Philippines.. So by my estimate, it would only take around ten million dollars to make these adorable little coffee creatures' lives quite bearable.

Chapter 7
Meeting the Middle Man and Mentor

I had only two main reasons to find myself in Ho Chi Minh City. One was to meet up with my coffee wholesaler; the other was to visit the Hard Rock Cafe Saigon. So I only scheduled myself to stay for two nights.

The flight to Saigon International Airport from Dalat lasted all of 45 minutes. Two and a half hours including checking into the flight, going through security, waiting for the flight, and waiting for my luggage when I got there. You know, the way air travel should go.

When I arrived at Saigon Airport, we were cattle-driven into a bus and carted to where we could collect our bags. Once I had accomplished that feat, I had to go through a check to make sure I had the right luggage. Then I was quickly asked if I needed a taxi by a girl standing behind a desk I didn't have any cash on me but I also needed a ride so I told her that I needed a taxi. She asked me where I was staying, and I had to power up my phone and wait for it to establish a data connection so I could find my confirmation email. When I was able to give her the information she needed, she then asked for 200,000 Dong. I told her I needed to find an ATM. So she escorted me to the money based arcade game. I pulled the money I needed out of my account, gave her what I owed for the ride, and she escorted me to the cab.

Leaving the airport, we had to stop at a toll booth where the driver paid half my fare for the toll. Shortly after that obstacle we were in downtown Ho Chi Minh City. It was 4:00 pm and the traffic was truly ridiculous. I thought traffic in Bangkok was bad; Bangkok was child's play compared to Saigon. There were tons of cars and for every car there were at least fifteen motorbikes. The craziest part was the intersections. It didn't matter which way anyone was going, they all just blended together like a traffic smoothie. The picture of Wylie Coyote jumbled up holding a bunch of different direction signs in no particular order comes to mind. Anyway, I was ecstatic that I wasn't driving.

It took about a half an hour until I was dropped off near an alley that led to my hotel. I entered and checked in and quickly found out that my room again was on the fifth floor. One thing is for sure, this trip helped me train for climbing a mountain. Luckily, they wouldn't let me carry my bags this time. That was a blessing.

Once I was situated in my room, I sent Michael, my wholesaler, a message to let him know I was in town. We made plans to meet at the Hard Rock the next day for lunch.

The next morning I woke up and started walking across town to meet up with Michael at the Hard Rock. It was about an hour walk to get there but I knew I would see some interesting things along the way. One thing that gets incredibly annoying in the bigger cities of Southeast Asia is how aggressive the motorbike taxi drivers can be; well, the massage girls too for that matter, but at least they are pleasant on the eyes. Basically, each time I walked by one of these drivers they would offer a taxi, which is okay, but when I politely declined, they asked "Where are you going?" Then, it doesn't matter if I told them or ignored them, they started following me, trying to convince me to let them tak me to I was going I quickly learned to just ignore them and keep moving. The girls are much more fun because they grab you and offer to go back to your hotel with you if you don't stop at their massage parlor.

About three-quarters of the way into my journey across town, I located the statue of Ho Chi Minh. It was a very impressive and life like bronze that stood around twenty feet tall. He wore the Vietnamese military greens and flip-flops on his feet with his right hand extended into the air. The statue stood in the middle of a very nice park with an intricate building it.

I arrived at the Hard Rock Cafe about fifteen minutes later though the establishment wouldn't open for another thirty minutes. The time quickly passed and they opened the doors. As I made my ceremonial way around checking out the memorabilia I found some pretty awesome things. They had a suit worn by John Lennon. The plaque said that they had this piece of history at the Hard Rock Saigon because his song "Give Peace a Chance" was the anti-war anthem during the Vietnam War. They also had one of the suit jackets that Dan Aykroyd wore while filming the Blues Brothers, as well as one of Jimi Hendrix' bandanas. There was also a softball uniform that Elvis Presley had worn during a police charity softball game in Memphis, Tennessee where his famous home Graceland is located. They had a lot of really great stuff at this Hard Rock location, but they also had something that broke my heart. They thought they had a guitar signed by my all-time favorite band Pantera, but it definitely was not signed by any of them.

Once my tour was complete, I went back into the bar and I ordered an iced tea and waited for Michael to arrive. I soon got a message that he was running late, and he had to mail a sample to a client and he would be there in about an hour. I sat and drank my tea and mused around on TripAdvisor looking for interesting things to go find on my way back towards the hotel.

About an hour and fifteen minutes later he finally arrived. He was very apologetic for keeping me waiting. We discussed coffee, business strategy, and business in general, and decided that I should ap-

ply for my state business license when I got back
the hotel to make it easier to import a large amount
of coffee I was getting ready to purchase, but I
should wait until I get home to buy it. This thinking
made a lot of sense. He also wondered about how I
was going to bag the coffee for sale after I roasted it.
I told him I had been researching the aluminum
bags with gas valves, but I would need a sealer. He
gave me an address to a place in Ho Chi Minh City
that sold them, and also offered to ship it to me
with my order. He told me that He could get me a
good deal on a larger coffee roaster when I was
ready for one. We spent about an hour and a half
together then parted ways.

When I left, I hailed a taxi and went to the address
that belonged to the company Tân Thanh Hưởng
Dẫn Sử Dung. All this company sells is sealing
products, and the one I was looking at, a pedal im-
pulse sealer, would only cost $53. I figured I was
going to spend at least $500 on one of these. Unfor-

tunately, they were unable to ship to the states. I asked for a catalog and told them that my friend would probably come buy it for me and ship it to me.

That night, I purchased a bag sealer on Amazon, and applied for my Washington State Business License under the name Ohm Coffee Tea & Spice, knowing I was going to need it when I got home so I could place my order. Both were waiting for me when I returned to the States.

Chapter 8
The Start-up...

I arrived at my house on a Friday afternoon. I went through the pile of mail that had built up over the last five weeks, hoping to find my business license. Unfortunately, I had to wait through the weekend until it finally showed up on Monday. I contacted Michael, the Vietnamese coffee wholesaler, and let him know I had my Unified Business Number. Then I placed my order for 540 kilograms of green Arabica coffee. He told me it would take a few days to prepare my order and invoice.

While I waited, I built my coffee bag sealing table and started putting together my packaging and marketing ideas. I began to focus on getting people to subscribe to a monthly bag of freshly roasted coffee. I had the idea that I should offer starter packs so that my customers would have the option of being able to get everything they need to brew their first cup of coffee. I did some research and purchased four of each of these items: an electric tea kettle, an electric grinder, and a French press coffee maker.

Then I turned to a website called gearbubble.com, which is a company that allows you to design things like t-shirts, coffee cups, key chains, and a lot of other things. They then allow you to set up a storefront website and name the pricing for the items you designed, down to what they need to get their profits out of the deal. I designed a color-changing coffee cup with the Ohm Coffee, Tea & Spice logo, and Gearbubble printed it to order. I set the price at $9.95 per cup. The suggested price was $19.95, but I was more interested in keeping the cost low so I could buy them whenever I needed them. Out of the $9.95, for every coffee cup that sold, I would get $3.95 in profits,. I ordered eight of the mugs.

My finished starter pack was a kettle, a grinder, a French press, two color-changing Ohm Coffee cups, and three half-pound packages of different roast profiles for the customer to decide which roast they wanted to receive a pound of every month. I planned to charge $99.95 for the starter package, then $30.00 a month for the subscription, which also included a monthly newsletter and free samples of any new product I added to my store.

I designed labels for the coffee bags and had a 100 of them printed at stickermule.com for $80. It wasn't the best price, but I wanted to get them quickly and I would worry about getting a much better price on stickers later.

Next, I turned my attention back to an affordable coffee roasting machine that could roast five pounds at a time. I'd been looking for about six months before I left for Hawaii and the cheapest I could find cost nearly $8000.00. But I kept looking and looking. I knew in my heart I would find something affordable to get started. When I returned from Hawaii, I just happened to look on eBay, where I found a coffee roaster machine that did everything I needed for $1400.00. Needless to say, I jumped on it

The roaster was pretty cool and ingenuitive. It was built out of a Ronco Turkey Rotisserie Oven. They had added a new heating element and a fan to it, as well as turning the rotisserie fork into a drum to turn the beans in. It was a pretty ingenious idea.

At this point, all I needed was to get the coffee paid for and delivered, and to install a chimney from my coffee roasting machine out of my garage, and I would be in business.

It took Michael an entire week to get back to me with the invoice, but he said my order was packed and ready to go. I purchased 540 Kilograms of green Arabica coffee shipped to my house for $2538.00; plus wire transfer fees and customs fees it totaled $3100. It was supposed to take five weeks to arrive at my door once payment is received.

But I had to figure out how to get the money to Vietnam. So, I went to my credit union and I was told that they do not do international wire transfers. Then I went to a local bank, and they said if I have an account they would do it for $45. All I would need to do is give them the invoice, pay the fee, and give them the money; and they would take care of the rest. So then I checked with the Western Union. They said they could do it for $27. I tried to make the transaction, and it was denied. I was getting frustrated. I talked to Michael again, and he said I would probably need to open a business account at a bank in order to make it happen. So the next morning I did just that, after stopping by my credit union and taking out $3000.00 cash to open the account. Once the account was opened, the payment was sent. Then I purchased the stuff I needed for the chimney. Now I had five weeks to get that installed. Once the shipment arrived, I would finally be able to sell a bag of coffee after working so diligently for two years trying to make this happen.

As you might recall from earlier in the book, when I was in Chiang Mai, Thailand, I purchased two kilograms of green coffee from a lady at Libernard Coffee. I ended up carrying it with me through all of Thailand, from the north to the south, and through all of Vietnam, from the south to the north. Finally, I brought it through Tokyo, Japan, and Vancouver, British Columbia Canada and into the United States. About a week before Christmas 2016, I finally had the coffee roaster installed in my garage. This well-traveled coffee ended up being the first roast for my coffee company. I ended up with eight half-pound bags of medium roast Thai Arabica that I announced for sale on Facebook. Within 24 hours, every last bag was sold for $15 per bag. I felt like I was definitely on to something.

A couple days after Christmas, I finally heard back from Michael, and my order still had not left Vietnam. He had forgotten to tell me that I needed an FDA number on the shipping documents. So, I had to go through the nightmare of having to figure out how to get that setup. This activity took a couple more weeks, and I was getting impatient with not having any coffee for sale. Meanwhile, Michael suggested that I order a micro-lot of some of the super rare Yellow Caturra, so I did and had it shipped airmail and received it about a week later. The coffee ended up costing me about $15 per pound after shipping, so I had to charge $25 for a half pound to make it worth my while. Luckily, I was able to market it for what it was, as being one of the world's rarest coffees. I ended up attending the Seattle Coffee Convention, and I took a little with me to let some of the pros try. I was told I should be selling it for $70 a pound!

Over the next couple of weeks, I needed to hire an import agent to get my order off of the boat from Vietnam. I kept calling different companies without any success. It was very stressful and annoying. Finally, three days before my shipment was scheduled to arrive, I found a company to be my agent. A few days later I got the call that I could come pick my order up at the port in Auburn, Washington. This meant that I needed to rent a U-Haul, and drive 120 miles round trip to pick up my coffee, but, at least it was stateside. So I did just that. I got to the port, and the people in the office told me that I didn't have the proper clearance to pick up my order. I called my agent, and it turned out they had forgotten to fax an important document. That took about 10 minutes, then the van was loaded with the half ton of coffee and I was on my way back home where my friend helped me load the 9 giant bags of coffee into my garage. After I returned the U-Haul, I fired up the roaster again.

Shortly after, in early February, Starbucks introduced a new product that was an oak whiskey barrel aged coffee from Sulawesi, Indonesia. It was only available at the Starbucks Private Reserve Roastery in Seattle, Washington. They only had 800 pounds and all of it that they had bagged for sale, sold in less than an hour. I took myself up there and got a pour over so I could try it. I was lucky enough to try it a few times.

Then I started researching it. I even attempted to interview the Starbucks roaster who developed it. That didn't work out, but I did end up finding out that it took Starbucks four years in research and development to create a sellable product. I started going around to all the local whiskey distilleries, hoping to find an oak whiskey barrel, so that I could try to create my own whiskey coffee. Soon, I found myself in Tacoma, Washington at Chambers Bay Whiskey Distilling Company. I talked them into donating three small barrels in which they had aged their product, Greenhorn Bourbon. When I got home, I found I could put 10 pounds of green coffee beans in a barrel. I loaded a barrel up and let it sit for a couple months.

The next two months were great! I went from selling a couple bags of coffee per day, to the point where I was regularly selling at least five. This culminated in April, the day before Easter, when I think I sold 23 bags of coffee. I had been using mostly Facebook for advertising, and I was inviting people over for a free cup of coffee. I would take their photo either sipping the coffee or holding a bag of coffee if they offered to buy some. Then I would post them on the Ohm Coffee Facebook page. I even ended up with a photo of Gilbert Gottfried holding a bag of my coffee. Things were going pretty well. Then, in the beginning of April, I removed a pound of the beans from the barrel, and roasted them just to see how it was coming. I could definitely taste the oak and the whiskey in the coffee, but it was still a really light aftertaste. I let it sit for a couple more weeks.

Chapter 9
Stumbling Blocks

Starting a business isn't always unicorn farts and hiking with munchkins. In fact, it can be downright torturous sometimes. You can be moving along thinking you are grabbing the world by the horns, then all of the sudden. Boom! You're sitting in a corner by yourself crying from the pain. This is especially true with a start-up business. I feel it's important to understand this before jumping into starting a business. Not because I want to discourage anyone from trying their hand (actually, I encourage everyone to go and achieve their goals and dreams,) but because being prepared with this knowledge will help you get through it.

It was nearly the middle of April of 2017. I was roasting a bunch of coffee (about 20 pounds) for a community garage sale I had just ordered a nicely branded banner so the people at the sale would get the feeling that Ohm Coffee, Tea, and Spice was a real business and not just some guy's garage hobby. I was feeling pretty good about myself, and I knew I would be hearing from the trademark office soon, as well.

The sale was the day before Easter, so I decided to put together a few Easter baskets, thinking it would be a great gift to give a coffee lover. It would include a pour-over kit and a pound of coffee. It came with a grinder, a carafe, a reusable filter, an electric kettle, and I even threw in a bunch of Easter candy in to fill it out. It was a $100 that would be well worth every penny. I put six of these together, which took most of the profits I had collected since I had been in business. It was a gamble that I felt pretty confident in. Once I put these baskets together, that is when my world began to crumble.

Sometimes, the way you run your business is completely affected by what is going on in your personal life. By "sometimes" I mean 100 percent of the time. When your personal life is going well, chances are you are making better decisions, mostly because you are not running into work to try to get a distraction.

About five days before the sale, I got word that my grandfather in Sioux Falls, South Dakota had fallen down and hit his head really bad, and my entire family was concerned that he might not make it. He had a really bad concussion, and at the age of 94, concussions are not an easy thing to recover from. I knew that I had to stick around for the sale, but I was going to jump in the car and drive across five states so I could see him one more time , as over my life I hadn't gotten a lot of time with my grandparents.

The day of the sale came, and I had gotten set up with the banner behind my table, and I had a pour over for each roast, and a French Press for the white coffee. I ended up selling half of what I had roasted that day, which was a disappointment, but even more disappointing, I didn't sell any of the Easter baskets. Another thing that I found was that the older generation that gravitated to a community garage sale were around the age of the people who had fought in Vietnam. I caught a lot of flak from some of the local Vietnam War Veterans like the coffee had shot at them in the war. I couldn't believe that they were that disgusted at my coffee just because of an unfortunate time in history. It was really sad to witness.

After the garage sale was over I loaded everything back into the car, and I was heading home to unload before my drive to South Dakota. Everything seemed to be going as planned, but when I went out to the car to leave, I had a flattening tire. It was late enough that all the tire places were closed. I decided I would change my spare, then go to Walmart in the morning (being Easter, the better tire shops were all closed.) In the morning, I went to Walmart, just to find out that the tire had a tiny little screw in it, but it was close enough to the sidewall that it wasn't repairable. I also found out that my car had an odd size tire, so it ended up costing me $150 to replace it, and that took a lot of what I was planning on using for the trip. It totally sucked, but I was getting a paycheck in a couple of days so I decided to wait to leave until it showed up.

The next day, I got a letter from the Trademark Office telling me that they couldn't issue me my trademark. As it turned out a company in California had filed a claim on the word "Ohm" in association with coffee a month earlier than when I filed. It hadn't even hit the computer yet, so there was no way I ever could have seen that coming. After talking to a lawyer later that day, I found that there was nothing I could do except change my name and lose all of the momenta I had built over the last few months.

The next day I found out that a phone company whose name is a six letter word with the definition "run at full speed over a short distance" had taken an extra $150 from my account for some ungodly reason, which I still to this day do not understand why. (Don't do business with them they are a terrible company.) Then, I ran over another tiny little screw, just like the last one. I'm pretty sure someone was planting. Luckily, I was able to get this one fixed. And I got another random bill that showed up. Just like that, I couldn't afford to go see my grandparents.

It wasn't all bad though. Not being able to drive east freed me up to go to the International Specialty Coffee Association Convention in Seattle.

I'm not going to talk much about the massive convention, but I did end up meeting a Brazilian Coffee Roaster, named Marcelo Franck from Franck's Ultra Coffee, who specializes in whiskey-barrel aging. In our conversation, he lovingly gave me the secret to making the whiskey coffee turn out the way I was looking for. On my way home from the convention, I stopped at Chambers Bay Whiskey, and got the final ingredient I needed to make it work correctly. When I got home I set a second batch to begin aging. When I pulled it a couple months later, it was perfect; even better than what I remember the Starbucks whiskey coffee tasting.

Now it was time to shift my focus towards finding a new name for my company and designing a new. It took me a while to come up with a new name, *Sassy's Exquisite*. I chose this when I looked up the word "Luxury" in Vietnamese. The Vietnamese word that came back was "Xa Xi" which is pronounced "Sassy" and I loved the idea! So I took the money I made from the garage sale and used it to file the trademark.

Meanwhile, I wasn't really able to do any advertising because I didn't want to infringe on the other company's trademark, and all of my stuff was already branded, so my sales quickly tanked.

While all of this was going on, the girl I was involved with began acting a bit strange, but I didn't really pay that much attention at the time. My mind was a million other places, needless to say, until we had a huge blowout. I was so upset, I nearly killed a guy who was involved in the mix. I put my foot down, and I didn't want anything to do with anyone. I quickly fell into a pretty nasty depression and I had no idea how I was going to make the whirlwind of the bullshit stop and revive my business.

Although I still had a few sales trickling in, but nowhere near what I really needed, I began really pressing. I started doing things in my business that didn't feel authentic, and I think my customer base felt that too because I continued to watch my sales diminish.

In mid-May, I went to a Kyle Cease Evolving Out Loud event at the Moore Theatre in Seattle, Washington. I knew that I would definitely get a refresh of my positive and authentic attitude, which I desperately needed. Halfway through the 2-hour event, I got a text from my aunt, telling me that my grandfather had just had a stroke. I just started crying while sitting in the audience. But I made the decision that I was no longer going to be the guy who couldn't afford to go see his grandparents. I was through playing the game of small-ball. It was time to start hitting homers again. This change in mindset worked! I started being true to myself again and I quickly noticed an uptick in my sales. That is until the end of the month when my family underwent a big change.

When I was in the first grade my father had tipped a forklift on himself at work and broke his back, leaving him paralyzed from the waist down. I'll spare this book the details, but it does affect this part of my story. He had been in the hospital and nursing homes for most of the prior 15 years dealing with a smattering of bed sores and a few strokes that occurred during a surgery that left him a 2-month long coma. Suddenly, at the end of May, he finally came home after I had fought tooth and nail for four years to make it possible because the nursing home he was in had to shut its doors and there was nowhere else for him to go. Unfortunately, no nursing or caregiving process had been put in place so over the next two weeks, I managed to get a part-time caregiver in place; however, the nursing help never came because his insurance company wasn't accepted by any of the local visiting nurse networks. Basically, I ended up under "house arrest" because he needed me there to take care of him. I definitely didn't have any time to work on my business, or anything for me, period.

Then one morning, I was awakened up by an adult protective services investigator who informed me I had been reported for neglect of an elder. In two weeks, because I couldn't get him any nursing, he went from being healthy enough to come home, to nearly going septic from the fast deterioration of his wounds. *But neglect?* I had to do what I had to do and called an ambulance to come pick him up.

I spent the next few weeks trying to get him moved from the hospital into a long-term facility. This too was a nightmare, which involved me threatening lawsuits to different companies. Of course, by the end of this month of complete hell, my business was driven completely into the ground. *Dead.*

Chapter 10
Rebooting the Dream

Literally, the day after I was finally able to get my father placed into a long-term nursing facility, my right rear molar broke. I couldn't believe it. The prior few months had been going as such that if something was possible to go wrong, it would do just that. Luckily, I was able to find a dentist that got me in for a root canal within an hour of the breakage. The dental work ended up costing me $1400 but it left me with a temporary filling in my drilled out tooth. It was going to cost another fortune to walk out of the office with a quality crown.

On my prior trip to Vietnam, I had spent the final two weeks in Hanoi, where I decided to get my smile fixed. I ended up getting ten fillings and three crowns for a total of what I had just paid for the root canal. I knew that I could fly to Hanoi, round-trip, stay for three weeks, and get the crown I needed for less than what it would cost to just get the crown replaced at home. I found and booked a round-trip ticket for less than $600.

The plan was to fly out of Seattle, Washington on September 5th, 2017 and return on September 25th. A couple days after I booked the trip, I looked at my reservation, and realized that I had booked the return for October 25th. Once I realized my mistake, I contacted Asiana Airlines to see if I could switch the flight. They told me that they could switch the flights for me but it was going to be a $300 fee plus any difference in ticket prices. I decided that I might as well stay in Southeast Asia for the extra month, considering the fact that it is much cheaper to live over there than it is to live in the States. Not only that, but I realized after everything I had been through recently, I really needed to go and reconnect with myself.

I spent the next couple of months just trying to help a buddy get his new brewpub running. At the time, I didn't really want to even think about what I felt was one of my worst failures in my life. But I was working on clearing out the rest of my roasted coffee stock. His pub "Flood Valley Brewing Craft Tap House" in Chehalis, Washington ended up becoming the first location where *Sassy's Exquisite* had a small retail booth.

When I finally left at the beginning of September, I flew to Hanoi. I landed at 9:00 pm and got checked in to my hotel. In the morning, I headed straight to the dentist to start the process of getting my tooth taken care of. I had to come back a couple days later to have it fitted. After that, I was without any agenda for my trip. I reconnected with the famous Vietnamese "egg coffee" at the Giang Cafe, a little hole in the wall that has been open since before the beginning of the Vietnamese Civil War. They were the ones who invented the national drink. On this trip,

I ended up finding out that there are two different styles of egg coffee. One style where they use the yoke of the egg is one of the best things I have ever experienced. Tasting the real Vietnamese egg coffee is something that should be on every coffee lover's bucket list. The other style of egg coffee uses the egg white instead of the yoke, and it isn't anywhere near as good. Way back before my first trip to Vietnam, with my class a few years earlier, I had seen Anthony Bourdain try egg coffee while he was in Hanoi, and I knew it was something I would have to seek out. When I was there, of course, I did just that. Though, I also paid the person who made it for me to teach me how to make it. In the next chapter, I will include some coffee recipes I have encountered in my travels around the world.

On this trip, I found another coffee drink that I had never heard about, banana coffee. I found this drink at a vegan restaurant called "The Veg." Not only was this banana coffee a wonderful concoction, but the food there is quite amazing as well.

A couple weeks later, I found myself in Dalat City, Vietnam where I met up with Lan and she took me to see her family again. Her family farm had grown up. She had added a $200,000.00 greenhouse, and she had purchased a couple new farms. It really helped my mindset to see how much my friend's business had grown over the year since I had been there. I stayed in Dalat for a few days, and then headed back to Ho Chi Minh City where I met up with Michael.

Michael sent a car to pick me up and it drove me an hour across the city. It dropped me off in an industrial area where they were building coffee roasting machines. I was just standing there hoping someone who spoke English would come talk to me, but this was to no avail. Yet, after a few minutes, one of the employees walked up to me and patted me on the shoulder and motioned for me to follow him. I ended up on the back of a motorbike, and he drove me a few minutes away to an office. There I was greeted by a man and a woman, and they spoke very little English, but I was asked to sit down in the office at the desk, which had one of the roasters they were building where I was originally dropped off.

My host told me Michael would be there soon, and he began to make some coffee to drink while I waited. When Michael arrived, he told me that they wanted to teach me how to use their machine, so I could be their agent in the United States. After they showed me how to use the machine, I ended up roasting coffee for the next six hours. When I left that day, Michael sent me on my way with a kilogram of the Mocha Arabica I had been roasting, and 10 kilograms of green Arabica pea berry, that I carried with me through Phnom Penh and Siem Reap, Cambodia, a flight to Bangkok, Thailand, a train ride to Koh Samui, Thailand, and a plane ride to Chiang Mai and eventually a car ride to Pai.

My first day in Chiang Mai, Thailand, I went back to see Bong at Libernard Coffee, the little shop where I had purchased the 2 kilograms of Thai green coffee the year before. I took some of each of my 2-ounce sample bags of coffee, a medium roast, a French roast, and an espresso roast, and I gave it to Bong as a gift. She was so excited. She didn't remember me at first, but then after a few minutes, she remembered when I had bought the green beans from her the last year. I spent a week in Chiang Mai except for the day I left to go to Pai, and I made sure to go to her shop every day. The day before I went to Pai, I purchased 10 Kilograms of green coffee from her, and she also helped me acquire the Thai color-changing flower tea. While I was in Pai, I shipped the 20 kilograms of green coffee I had picked up during my adventure. Then I began my week-long trip back home. When I got home, I was back in a beautiful mindset again, and I was ready to take on the world once more.

That brings me to the current time where I'm writing this book, and the end of the story to this point. 2018 is about rebuilding everything I had lost in April, May, and June, but in a much stronger and successful way.

Chapter 11
Roasts and Recipes

There are tons of different ways to enjoy coffee. In this chapter, I am going to explain many of these drinks, as well as give the recipes to make them. A lot of this chapter is based on research, however, some of what we are going to find here comes from the exotic things I have found while traveling the world, whether it be somewhere in Southeast Asia or China, Rome, or Egypt. In different parts of the world, they do different but interesting things with their coffee. As you read this chapter, feel free to grab your favorite Sassy's Exquisite roast and try any drink that piques your interests.

I'm going to start this list with the drinks I think most are aware of, but what most are unaware of, is the actual formulas for preparing them correctly. My goal here is to teach how to prepare that coffee shop quality coffee in the comfort of your home or office.

But before I get to that, I want to explain the differences in roast profiles:

Green Unroasted Coffee

This, I think, is pretty much self-explanatory. The coffee beans are unroasted and green, so haven't had a chance to release any oil or moisture, and the beans are very small and compact. It has the highest caffeine content it will ever have, but good luck grinding it! It will more than likely break your grinder. However, if you are able to get it ground, it's going to taste like grass soup.

White Coffee

White coffee is barely roasted. It has a yellowish color to it and the beans are still very hard. If you use your grinder to grind white coffee, you might as well retire it from grinding darker roasts because you won't be able to grind with precision anymore. That being said, white coffee needs a coarse grind so it will work fine for that. White coffee is super high in caffeine content, but it doesn't taste like coffee at all. In fact, it smells and tastes like peanuts. It is commonly referred to as coffee for people who want the zoom but don't like coffee. It also makes a great pre-workout drink, because the natural caffeine high is sure to launch you into the stratosphere.

Light, or Cinnamon, Roast

When roasting coffee, once the temperature of the beans get to a certain point, usually between 400°F and 410°F, they start to crack and pop like really loud Rice Krispies. If the roaster pulls the batch at around 390°F the beans will have a light brown color to them, but they still haven't gotten to that first crack stage. This is the roast profile for people who really want that caffeine buzz but also enjoy the flavor of coffee because the flavor we all recognize is the caramelization of the bean's natural oils.

Medium Roast, City Roast, Vienna Roast

This roast profile is pulled just after the beans' first crack, as mentioned above, which is used by coffee-sommeliers in most coffee grower/roaster competitions. At this profile, you get a good bang from the caffeine content, and you get to taste all the interesting flavor nuances the bean has to show. This is by far my favorite roast profile, and I prefer not roasting past this profile when I am roasting something really special like a Kopi Luwak or a yellow Caturra or something else really rare.

Medium Dark Roast, Full-City Roast, Vietnamese Roast

I spoke earlier about the first crack that takes place between 400°F and 410°F, but there is a second crack temperature, usually between 435°F and 450°F. When the batch is pulled at about 430°F, or just prior to the second crack, it's at a medium dark roast. Of course, it is quite a bit darker than the medium, but it's a little easier on the caffeine, and the flavor is a bit more robust with fewer nuances. The caramelization is a bit heavier and the flavor from that is beginning to take over.

French Roast

French Roast occurs just after the second crack. When this happens the bean starts to heavily release its natural oils that have caramelized during the roast. After it has had a day or so to rest after being roasted, it takes on an oily sheen. It is a fairly dark roast and most of the people who grew up drinking coffee from a can tend to adore this profile. Again it had a very full-bodied and robust flavor, but it has less of a caffeine kick to it.

Espresso Roast, Italian Roast

This profile occurs when roasting bit longer after the second crack, giving the newly released oils time to caramelize on the outside of the bean. This is the roast most commonly served in Italy and most Espresso shops around the world. It can be quite a shock to the taste buds if sipped without sugar due to its robust and whole-bodied flavor, but it has even less caffeine content than the French Roast.

Spanish Roast

I honestly do not understand why anyone would want this. It is roasted so dark that it is pulled moments away from catching on fire. It is literally on the verge of being charcoal instead of coffee. It tastes like smoke and it has almost no caffeine content. Sassy's Exquisite does not roast this profile.

Now to the recipes . . .

Drip Coffee

Most people have that automatic drip coffee maker sitting somewhere in their kitchen. It is usually a bulky machine made of plastic with a large glass pot designed to catch the brewed coffee after it passes from the water reservoir through the ground coffee and the filter. Most aficionados ridicule the automatic drip machines because it just doesn't extract the coffee grounds the way the grounds deserve to be extracted. But these machines are perfect for when you are drinking cheap coffee, like Folgers or Yuban. I'm not saying they are unable to make good coffee, or that cheap coffee like Folgers or Yuban is terrible coffee. However, by following a few guidelines, you can come away with better

Here are the tools that are needed:

- Automatic Drip Coffee Machine
- Coffee Filter for said machine
- 7-gram Measuring Spoon
- Kitchen Scale
- Purified Drinking Water
- Coffee

Directions

First things first: Decide how many cups of coffee to brew. This is a very important part of the process. Its always better to brew less than needed, because we can always brew more. This recipe is for a single cup of coffee. To make more, just do the math for 2 cups: use this recipe x2. To make 8 cups, use this recipe x8. It's fairly simple.

There is a "Golden Ratio" for brewing coffee:
1 Tablespoon of coffee (7 grams)
6 ounces of water (168 grams)

Place the coffee pot on the kitchen scale and add the water until it reaches the desired weight. Then pour it into the reservoir. If using a lesser quality machine, turn it on and run the water through once, then pour it back into the reservoir so it can actually get the temperature up to where it needs to be. We want our coffee to brew between 200°F and 205°F, not quite boiling, but very close.

Take 7 grams of whole bean coffee (best because it stays fresh longer) and grind it) preferably in a burr or mill grinder. I know they are more expensive, but the extra $80-$100 spent on the good grinder as opposed to the $15 blade grinder makes all the difference in the world when it comes to that first sip. The coarseness of the grind also makes a huge difference. If the grind is too fine, it will not only make a bitterer cup of coffee from over-extraction, but it will also more than likely clog the filter. This could end up becoming very messy while using an automatic drip machine, because the water with the coffee grounds in it will leak all over the counter. If the brew ends up too light, or flat tasting, it's because the grind is too coarse, and will have mostly water in your cup because the coffee grounds are under-extracted. It may be necessary to play with the grinder a little bit to find the proper medium.

Once the beans are ground, put them in the filter, put the filter back in the machine, and the coffee pot where it is supposed to go, turn on the machine and let it make coffee. When the drip finishes, pour and enjoy.

French Press

The French Press: loved by many, despised by few. The French Press is great for the on-the-go coffee drinker who enjoys a bold, full-bodied cup of coffee. In my opinion, the only real drawback to the device is that it leaves a coffee mud in your cup.

What is a French Press? It is a cylindrical vessel, with a handle, a lid that has a screen filter that snuggly fits the width of the opening, and a plunger coming out of the top of the lid. The French press is usually made out of glass, though sometimes we can find one that is made of stainless steel. **<u>Here are the tools that are needed:</u>**

- 3-cup French Press
- 7-gram Measuring Spoon
- Kitchen Scale
- Some sort of Tea Kettle
- Purified Drinking Water
- Coffee

Directions

For the average 3-cup press, scoop up 21-28 grams of your favorite Sassy's Exquisite Coffee. (We do not recommend our Oak Whiskey Barrel Aged Coffee for this method, but we do highly recommend our Vietnamese White.) Grind it to a coarse grind. Then add it to the press. Heat the purified drinking water to between 200°F and 205°F, which is not quite boiling, but very close. Place the press on the kitchen scale and zero the scale out. Then pour 150 grams of the heated water into the press and wait 30 seconds. Give the coffee a quick stir then add more water until it reaches 290-300 grams. Place the plunger-lid on the press and let the coffee steep for

4 minutes. At the 4 minute mark press the plunger down and immediately serve. (For darker roast, plunge a little earlier. For lighter roast, wait a little longer. If using the Vietnamese White, steep for 10 minutes), If there is still some coffee left in the press after serving, pour the remaining java into an insulated cup or thermos, so it remains hot and fresh and doesn't continue to extract from the grounds and get bitter.

Pour-Over

The Pour-Over is easily my favorite way to brew a cup of coffee. The Pour-Over is basically a manual drip coffee. In my opinion, it is the best way to get a great extraction, and it is also probably the fastest way to start sipping in the morning, unless you have a drip machine on a timer! So what exactly is a Pour-Over? Well, The Pour-Over is brewed in a carafe with a filter. Depending on the maker, the carafes use different types of filters. For instance, the world-famous Chemex Pour-Over uses a paper filter, while Bodum uses a reusable metal filter.

Here are the tools that are needed:

- Pour-Over Carafe
- Coffee Filter for said Pour-Over Carafe
- 7-gram Measuring Spoon
- Kitchen Scale
- Some sort of Tea Kettle
- Purified Drinking Water
- Coffee

Directions

Scoop out 21-28 grams of your favorite Sassy's Exquisite coffee (We do not recommend our Vietnamese White.) Grind the coffee coarsely where the grounds resemble the size of salt or sugar crystals. Pour the grounds into the filter and level (If using a paper filter, lightly wet the filter in the carafe, then discard the water before adding the grounds.) In the kettle heat 600 grams of purified drinking water to between 200°F and 205°F. Once the grounds are in the filter and the filter is placed in the top of the carafe, place the carafe on the scale and zero it out. Slowly begin to pour the water into the grounds until all the grounds have become damp. The scale should read right around 60 grams. Wait about 30 seconds for the coffee to expand which will turn the grounds into a pre-filter. This stage is called the "Bloom." What is actually happening here is the coffee is releasing the carbon dioxide. Once this has taken place, again slowly begin to pour the hot water over the grounds in a circular motion from center to the edge of the grounds, making sure you have contact with the coffee grounds the entire pour. As the filter begins to fill with water, the scale should read around 150 grams; stop pouring and allow it to drain, then repeat up to 250 grams. Use the water to release the grounds from the side of the filter back into the center, to ensure an even extraction. Then pour once more until the scale reaches 350 grams or when the bubble at the bottom of the carafe is about half full of coffee, remove the filter, swirl the carafe around a little bit to give it a little bit of a mix and serve.

Vacuum Siphon

The Vacuum Siphon is one of the most wonderful ways to enjoy some amazing coffee by providing the best of both worlds between the French Press and the Pour-Over. It is definitely the method of choice for the coffee connoisseur and frequently used to brew the most expensive coffees in the world, such as Kopi Luwak. The only real drawback to this style is it takes forever to get a cup of coffee.

So what exactly is a Vacuum Siphon? Usually, it is a class bubble beaker with another glass piece sitting on top of it with a glass tube hanging into the middle of the bubble. The top piece has a chain-weighted filter that sits just above the glass tube with the chain dangling down the tube with a Bunsen burner under the bubble to make it all work.

<u>Here are the tools that are needed:</u>

- Vacuum Siphon Coffee Maker
- Coffee Filter for said Vacuum Siphon
- 7-gram Measuring Spoon
- Some sort of Kettle (To save time)
- Purified Drinking Water
- Coffee

Directions

In the kettle heat the water to about 190°F. Pour the water into the bubble beaker until it is about 3/4 full. Light the Bunsen burner and place it in the bubble beaker. Place the tube of the top piece into the bubble beaker, and the dangle the chain of the weighted filter down the tube, making sure the filter sits in the bottom of the glass snugly. Grind 21-28 grams of your favorite Sassy's Exquisite coffee (Vietnamese White not recommended, but our Oak Whiskey Barrel Aged Coffee really shines with this method,) and grind to in between coarse and fine. Pour the grounds on top of the filter and level them out evenly. Now, wait until the Bunsen burner heats the water up to a near boil. When this happens it will create a vacuum and it will force the water up the tube through the filter and the coffee grounds, filling the top part of the siphon. When all the grounds are covered in water, give the grounds a quick stir to ensure proper extraction. The coffee will steep in the top part of the siphon until the liquid begins to cool off. Once this happens, the coffee will head back down through the coffee grounds, the filter, and the tube into the bubble beaker. Remove and extinguish the Bunsen burner. Remove the top glass piece from the bubble and serve the coffee.

Espresso

Espresso and all the drinks that are made from it I suggest leaving to the professionals. Not because, I don't think anyone can make it, but because, most home espresso machines are junk, and don't do the coffee its justice. However, there are a few really good, but expensive, home espresso machines. I honestly don't know a lot about making espresso but I will impart what I do know.

<u>Here are the tools that are needed:</u>

- Espresso Machine
- Porta-filter
- Tamping device
- 2 shot glasses
- Purified Drinking Water
- Coffee

<u>Directions</u>

For espresso, it is important that you have a fine grind. In my experience, it makes for a better shot if it is ground just prior to extraction. So grind your favorite Sassy's Exquisite Coffee (We recommend Vietnamese Full-City, French, or Espresso Roast. The Vietnamese White is also great but it has a slightly different brewing method.) Fill the porta-filter with the coffee grounds (21-24 grams) and tamp it so it forms a cake of coffee grounds. (With the Vietnamese White do not tamp it down, just level it out with the top of the porta-filter and leave it loose.) Then affix the porta-filter to the espresso machine and use the machine as its instructions direct, making sure to catch the espresso in the shot glasses. Then immediately pour the shots into a cup and serve. If done properly, there will be a layer of crema on the top of the dark shot of coffee. If using white coffee, immediately remove the porta-filter, because its continued expansion can actually break your machine. You can get twice as much serveable coffee out of a porta-filter full of white coffee than from the darker roasts.

Following are a variety of espresso drinks:

Espresso Romano

This drink is usually only found in Italy and it is very good; after all, it's the Italians who perfected the espresso. So when making the Espresso Romano, follow the same instructions for making a shot of Espresso, except when serving, add a teaspoon of organic cane sugar and a wedge of lemon. The sugar and lemon turn the regular shot into a totally different experience altogether.

Ristretto

Ristretto is the little sibling of Espresso, because you use the same equipment and the same amount of coffee in the same way. The only difference is to use about half as much hot water when pulling the shot. For some reason, the result is a more full-bodied and less bitter, and sweeter flavor than an espresso shot, but less coffee to drink.

Americano

The Americano is just an espresso with more hot water added to it. Usually, a double shot of espresso is used and either 8-12 ounces of extra, hot water is added. For a triple shot Americano, add 16 ounces of water; use 20 oz. of water for a quad-shot Americano.

Long Black

The Long Black is the exact reverse of the Americano made by adding the espresso to the water.

Latte

This is usually a double shot of espresso mixed together with 8-12 ounces of steamed milk, but be sure not to steam the milk into a foam. The latte is most commonly served with flavored sugar syrups which kind of turns the drink into a hot milkshake , most commonly served is the Mocha, which is a chocolate latte.

Flat White

White Coffee is often confused with a latte or a cappuccino, and by an untrained coffee snob, it's a common mistake, but there is a difference between all three drinks. The Flat White Coffee is a double shot of Ristretto (60ml), with 120ml of steamed milk and then a micro-foam layered in the cup. Micro-Foam is a frothed milk that between the foam on a cappuccino and the steamed milk in a latte. Micro-foam has larger bubbles than the cappuccino foam does, but it doesn't have as much froth to it.

Cappuccino

A Cappuccino is a coffee drink made using a double shot of espresso (60ml), with 60ml of steamed milk, then 60ml of heavy foam layered on top. The 3 drinks are not much different, but they are all different.

Affogato

An Affogato is a double shot of espresso poured over a scoop of vanilla ice cream.

Macchiato

A Macchiato is a double shot of espresso with a dollop of heavy foamed milk. In the United States, the drink that Starbucks made famous as a Caramel Macchiato is totally different. It's actually more of a layered latte.

Dirty Chai

A Dirty Chai is a latte mixed with a spiced chai tea mixture. Frequently, a Chai Latte is just the chai mixture (sans coffee) mixed in with the steamed milk, but a Dirty Chai has the Espresso added as well.

Breve

A Breve is a latte or macchiato made with Half and Half instead of milk.

Frappe

The Frappe is a Latte blended with ice that ends up kind of resembling a milkshake or slushy.

Red Eye, Black Eye, Dead Eye, Lazy Eye

A lot of people do not know that coffee has four eyes. They are the Red Eye, which is a 1-ounce shot of Espresso added to 4 ounces of drip coffee. The Black Eye, which is a 2-ounce shot of Espresso added to 4 ounces of drip coffee. The Dead Eye, which is 3 ounces of Espresso added to 4 ounces of drip coffee. Then there is the Lazy Eye, which is a 2 ounce shot of espresso added to 4 ounces of decaffeinated drip coffee.

Vienna

A Vienna Style Espresso is a 2-ounce Espresso shot covered with whipped cream.

Borgia

The Borgia is a fairly uncommon drink made of a 2-ounce Espresso shot with hot chocolate added to it, which is then topped with whipped cream, cinnamon, and orange zest.

Turkish Coffee

Turkish Coffee is one of the oldest ways to make a cup of coffee. It is very stout, and it uses a lot of equipment that most people don't have. Traditionally, the super-finely hand-ground coffee is added to a hand-made small copper vessel that has a flared bottom. Then add water and place the bottom of the vessel into a bed of super-hot sand and wait for the coffee to boil to the top of the vessel. Then remove it from the sand and serve before drinking the Turkish Coffee, allow it to settle for a few minutes, which not only allows the grounds to settle to the bottom of the cup, but it also allows the flavor of the coffee to mature as it slightly cools off.

Today, Turkish Coffee can be made with Bunsen burners, however, the correct grinder, hand-made copper/silver vessels, and burners can easily cost up to $700 US.

Irish Coffee

To make a traditional Irish Coffee, add a teaspoon of brown sugar to the bottom of a coffee cup, then you add 4 ounces of French Press Brewed Coffee (We recommend the Sassy's Exquisite Oak Whiskey Barrel Aged Coffee), Then add a 2-ounce shot of your favorite Irish Whiskey, and top it with 2.5 ounces of heavy cream.

Mazagran

This is another really unique drink In a cup add some ice, then a swig of lemon juice, and a teaspoon of brown sugar, and some French pressed coffee to fill the cup.

Vietnamese Coffee

The Vietnamese traditionally drink Robusta coffee, which is normally higher in caffeine, and bitterness. It is usually roasted to a full-city roast profile, with soy sauce added to the beans while roasting.

When they drink their coffee, they normally add a tablespoon of sweetened condensed milk to the coffee to counteract the bitterness of the bean. **Egg Coffee** There are two styles of Egg Coffee. One I have found to be one of the truly best things I have ever experienced. The other is terrible, in my opinion.

Vietnamese Yoke

This style of coffee is the National drink of Vietnam. If you ever taste it, you will understand why it has this honor. I ran into this for the first time In Hanoi Vietnam the first time I visited. It was so good that I paid the person who made it for me to teach me how to make it. And now I am going to give this secret to you.

Here are the tools that are needed:

- Electric hand blender with detachable beaters
- A cup large enough for the beaters
- Cocoa powder duster
- 1 egg yolk
- Sugar
- Sweetened condensed milk
- Small coffee cup
- Cocoa powder

- Coffee brewed as you desire.

Put the egg yolk and desired amount of sugar into a blending container and use the blender to whip the yolk mixture until it becomes the consistency of pancake batter. Add a teaspoon or two of the sweetened condensed milk to the coffee cup then pour the egg yolk mixture into the cup as well; add coffee until the cup is full. Dust the top with cocoa powder and serve with a spoon. It can also be poured over ice for a completely different experience.

Vietnamese Egg White

I am not impressed with this style of egg coffee. It is more of a layered drink than its yoke up counterpart. To make this, it is much like preparing the egg yolk variety except use the egg white instead and you add it to the sugar and beat it until it becomes a meringue. Add a tablespoon or 2 of sweetened condensed milk to the bottom of a tall, thin, clear glass, then you add the coffee, and top it with the egg white mixture.

Banana Coffee

This drink is one that caught me by surprise. I was in a vegan restaurant named The Veg, in Hanoi, Vietnam when I saw this on their menu. I was curious so I ordered it and I am glad I did.

Take 2 small frozen bananas and put them in a blender, add 2 ounces of espresso and a couple pumps of chocolate syrup and a couple tablespoons of sweetened condensed milk, blend to a silky smooth texture and serve.

Butter Coffee

Down in Peru, they have been adding butter to their coffee for a long time. I found out about this in 2014 when my Spanish teacher told me about it. So, of course, I had to try it. Basically, put a couple tablespoons of unsalted cream butter (preferably from grass fed animals) in a blender, add the hot coffee and some hot water as if making a blended Americano (not that there is such a thing). Blending it all together mixes the butter into the coffee and makes it look like a latte, but it is so much tastier.

Bulletproof Coffee

Bulletproof Coffee is a company created by a man named Dave Astbury. He went to Tibet and someone had him try Yak Butter coffee. He fell in love. He came back to the United States and started researching and found that if the butter comes from animals that are not fed grains, then it becomes a powerful tool in weight loss and energy. He found that if mixed with Coconut MCT oil and by cutting the carbs from your diet, it supercharges these results. So he built his company called Bulletproof Coffee. They have a bunch of product lines, including their own coffee, their own butter and Ghee, and MTC Oil. They claim theirs is the best for making their flagship drink; however, I have made it with Kerrygold butter, and generic MTC oil, and I lost 35 pounds in a month and a half by drinking it every morning.

Directions

Take 2 tablespoons of butter produced from grass-fed cow's milk and combine it in a blender with 2 tablespoons of Coconut MTC oil. Add some organic stevia leaf power (green not the white stuff) if you want bulletproof to be sweetened. Then add the hot coffee and blend it for about 30 seconds then serve.

In conclusion . . .

I'm sure there are many, many more coffee drinks out there in the world, but I have not experienced them yet. Hopefully someday, I will be able to update this book with more. As for now, I want to thank you for taking the time to read my first book. I am truly grateful and I hope you enjoyed all the work I put into creating it. *Thank you!*

For speaking engagements or any other types of business, please email <u>sassysexquisite@gmail.com</u> *with inquires. Thank you*

www.ingramcontent.com/pod-product-compliance
Lightning Source LLC
Chambersburg PA
CBHW070546220526
45467CB00003B/1083